Grade 5

Addison-Wesley Mathematics

Practice Workbook

▲▼ Addison-Wesley Publishing Company

Menlo Park, California ■ Reading, Massachusetts ■ New York
Don Mills, Ontario ■ Wokingham, England ■ Amsterdam ■ Bonn
Sydney ■ Singapore ■ Tokyo ■ Madrid ■ San Juan

ISBN 0-201-27503-1   Text printed on recycled paper.

14 15 16 17 18 19 20 - HC - 95 94

Table of Contents

Name _____

Understanding Numbers

Express the mathematical symbols in words.

1. $16 + 8$ _____

2. $30 \div 10$ _____

3. $\frac{1}{3}$ _____

4. $60 - 56$ _____

Ring the correct symbols for the math words.
More than one choice may be correct.

5. seventy-two divided by six

   A $\frac{72}{6}$ B $\frac{6}{72} - 72$ C $72 \div 6$

6. twenty-seven less than fifty-three

   A $27 - 53$ B $53 - 27$ C $27 + 53$

7. eighteen more than twelve

   A $12 + 18$ B $18 > 12$ C $18 + 12$

8. two thirds

   A $\frac{3}{2}$ B $\frac{2}{3}$ C 2×3

Write each numerical expression using symbols.

9. fifty-six divided by eight _____

10. the sum of thirty-five and fifteen _____

11. forty-three less than ninety _____

12. five sixths _____

13. the product of two and nineteen _____

Number Properties

Write which property—commutative or associative—
tells you that each expression names the same number.

1. $(33 + 7) + 5 = 33 + (7 + 5)$ _____

2. $6 \times 30 = 30 \times 6$ _____

3. $18 + (22 + 10) = (18 + 22) + 10$ _____

4. $9 + 6 = 6 + 9$ _____

5. $(3 \times 2) \times 4 = 3 \times (2 \times 4)$ _____

6. $10 \times (6 \times 5) = (10 \times 6) \times 5$ _____

Find the value of each expression.

7. $(14 + 6) \times 2$ _____

8. $14 + (6 \times 2)$ _____

9. $3 + (5 \times 3)$ _____

10. $(3 + 5) \times 3$ _____

11. $8 + (2 \times 4)$ _____

12. $(8 + 2) \times 4$ _____

13. $(5 \times 6) + 3$ _____

14. $5 \times (6 + 3)$ _____

15. $(4 \times 5) + 10$ _____

16. $4 \times (5 + 10)$ _____

17. $(19 + 1) \times 5$ _____

18. $19 + (1 \times 5)$ _____

19. $(4 \times 5) + 5$ _____

20. $4 \times (5 \times 5)$ _____

21. $(6 + 2) \times 3$ _____

22. $6 + (2 \times 3)$ _____

23. $(7 \times 9) + 1$ _____

24. $7 \times (9 + 1)$ _____

25. $(4 \times 4) + 4$ _____

26. $4 \times (4 + 4)$ _____

Using Compatible Numbers

Show how you would order and group the numbers
to make it easy to find the sums and products.
Then solve using mental math.

1. $4 + 5 + 6$ _____

2. $2 \times 13 \times 5$ _____

3. $10 \times 17 \times 10$ _____

4. $32 + 6 + 8$ _____

5. $5 \times 19 \times 2$ _____

6. $41 + 16 + 9$ _____

7. $5 \times 18 \times 20$ _____

8. $3 + 8 + 17 + 22$ _____

9. $9 + 2 + 1 + 8$ _____

10. $12 + 19 + 11 + 18$ _____

11. $96 + 13 + 4 + 2$ _____

12. $4 \times 50 \times 6 \times 2$ _____

13. $4 \times 6 \times 25 \times 2$ _____

14. $43 + 12 + 7 + 8$ _____

15. $56 + 3 + 4 + 2$ _____

16. $7 \times 5 \times 9 \times 2$ _____

17. $20 \times 4 \times 5 \times 7$ _____

Understanding the Operations

Name the operation you need to use. Then solve.

1. Christine jogs 24 miles each week. This is 2 times as far as she ran when she started jogging. How far did Christine run each week when she first began jogging?

_____

2. The 12 players on the team chipped in $3 each to buy the coach a thank-you present. How much did they collect?

_____

3. David spent $2 on a frozen yogurt and still had $8 left. How much money did he have before he bought the yogurt?

_____

4. Fifth graders learn 19 new spelling words each week. This week Michele has 3 more to learn. How many spelling words has Michele learned?

_____

5. Maria puts 8 stickers on a page in her album. She has 64 stickers. How many album pages can she fill?

_____

6. John is going to a tennis camp that is a 2-hour drive from his house. His parents will make two round trips taking him to and from camp. How many hours will they drive?

_____

7. Robert has been rafting 9 times. His older sister, Julia, has gone on all of Robert's trips and has been on 3 additional trips. How many times has Julia been rafting?

_____

8. Helen had saved $9 for a pair of gloves. She found them on sale for $5. How much did she save by buying the gloves on sale?

_____

Exploring Algebra: Understanding Variables

Use the list below. Write the number property next
to the equation that matches it.

Zero Property of Addition.   Zero Property of Multiplication

Zero Property of Subtraction   One Property of Multiplication

1. $4 \times 1 = 4$ _____

2. $4 \times 0 = 0$ _____

3. $4 - 0 = 4$ _____

4. $4 + 0 = 4$ _____

In the problems below, first figure out what number
each variable stands for. Then complete each box to
answer the state quiz question.

5. Each variable in the equations stands for one of
these numbers: 1, 2, 4, or 5.
Question: What state is called the "Last Frontier"?

$A \times A = A$
$L \times L = S$
$K - A = S$

___	___	___	___	___	___
1	2	1	4	5	1

6. Each variable in the equations stands for one of
these numbers: 0, 1, 2, 4, 5, or 9.
Question: What state is called the "Peach State"?

$E \times E = E$
$E - G = E$
$A + A = O$
$O + E = I$
$R - I = O$

___	___	___	___	___	___	___
0	1	4	9	0	5	2

Using Critical Thinking

Give the next three numbers in each pattern.
Name the pattern.

1. 0, 3, 6, 9, _____,_____,_____

2. 25, 50, 75, 100, _____,_____,_____

3. 17, 22, 27, 32, _____,_____,_____

4. 98, 96, 94, 92, _____,_____,_____

5. 77, 66, 55, 44, _____,_____,_____

6. 0, 12, 24, 36, _____,_____,_____

7. 0, 1, 3, 7, _____,_____,_____

8. 0, 2, 6, 12, _____,_____,_____

Look for a pattern. Give the next two numbers.

9.

Length of an Edge in Units	Volume of the Cube in Cubic Units
1	1
2	8
3	27
4	_____
5	_____

10.

Number of Players	Teams
15	1
30	2
45	3
60	_____
75	_____

11.

Length of a Side in Units	Perimeter of the Square in Units
1	4
2	8
3	12
4	_____
5	_____

12.

Number of Weeks	Savings
1	$3
2	$6
3	$9
4	_____
5	_____

Name _____

Problem Solving: Introduction

Circle the letter of the numerical expression you
would use to solve the problem.

1. Last year Mattie spent $56 on film
for her camera. This year she spent
twice that amount. How much did
Mattie spend on film this year?

   A $56 − 2   **B** $56 × 2

2. Richard had 72 photographs in his
first album and 56 photographs in his
second album. How many photographs
did he have in both albums?

   A 72 + 56   **B** 72 − 56

Circle the letter of the numerical expression you
would use to solve the problem. Then solve.

3. Mary used 4 rolls of film. Each roll
had 36 exposures. How many
photographs did she take?

   A 36 ÷ 4   **B** 36 × 4

_____

4. 60 students shared 15 work tables at
the hobby fair. How many students
sat at each table?

   A 60 × 15   **B** 60 ÷ 15

_____

5. Jenna saved $12 by buying her camera
on sale. The regular price of the
camera was $75. How much did
Jenna spend?

   A $75 + $12   **B** $75 − $12

_____

6. Brandon bought a rocket model kit
for $36. Russell bought a kit for
$28. How much more did Brandon
pay for his rocket kit?

   A $36 + $28   **B** $36 − $28

_____

7. Last year 43 students participated in
the math fair. This year 59 students
participated. How many more students
participated this year?

   A 59 − 43   **B** 59 + 43

_____

8. On Monday Grace solved 17 of the
math contest challenge problems. On
Tuesday she solved 14 more. How
many did she solve altogether?

   A 17 − 14   **B** 17 + 14

_____

Deciding When to Estimate

Tell whether you can estimate the answer or whether you need to find an exact answer.

1. Film cost $3.99 a roll. Wes needed 3 rolls to take pictures at the class party. He had $15. Did Wes have enough money?

_____

2. Most of the 32 students donated $2 to help buy an encyclopedia set for the library. About how much did the class contribute?

_____

3. There are 32 students in the class. Pam baked 3 dozen muffins. If she gave each student 1 muffin, how many did she have left for the teachers?

_____

4. Students were required to complete a set of 14 math puzzles by Thursday afternoon. On Monday, Damon had completed 9 puzzles. How many more did he need to finish?

_____

5. Eric bought pretzels for $1.89, peanuts for $2.39, and popcorn for $0.99. How much did he spend?

_____

6. Flowers cost $5.99 a dozen. Rachel and Annie wanted to buy 2 dozen. They had $10. Did they have enough?

_____

7. The party was scheduled to last 1 hour. Mrs. Cobb wanted to show a video of the class trip that would take 10 or 15 minutes. About how much time would be left for other activites?

_____

8. Each math puzzle took Misty about a $\frac{1}{2}$ hour to complete. About how many hours did she spend on the full set of 14 puzzles?

_____

9. Mr. Richards bought balloons for decorations. The packages contained from 7 to 9 balloons. If he bought 5 packages, about how many balloons did he buy?

_____

10. Joseph collected stickers. He realized he had just enough doubles to give everyone in the class 3 stickers. How many extra stickers did Joseph have?

_____

Name _____

Place Value Through Thousands

Write the numbers from the box that have:

| 492 |
| 6,357 |
| 5,968 |
| 26,846 |
| 45,183 |
| 50,406 |
| 634,582 |
| 572,031 |

1. 8 in the tens place _____

2. 6 in the hundred thousands place _____

3. 5 in the thousands place _____

4. 4 in the hundreds place _____

5. 7 in the ten thousands place _____

Write each number in standard form.

6. $50,000 + 400 + 20 + 8$ _____

7. $200,000 + 6,000 + 90 + 1$ _____

8. fifteen thousand, three hundred twenty-one _____

9. sixty-four thousand, thirty-seven _____

10. two hundred ninety-five thousand, eight hundred sixty-four _____

Write each number in expanded form.

11. 4,362 _____

12. 28,567 _____

13. 49,081 _____

14. 529,680 _____

15. 670,415 _____

Name _____

Millions and Billions

Write the digit that is in each place in this number.

563,201,897

1. ones _____   **2.** hundred millions _____   **3.** thousands _____

4. ten millions _____   **5.** hundreds _____   **6.** ten thousands _____

7. tens _____   **8.** hundreds thousands _____   **9.** millions _____

Write each number in standard form.

10. billions period: 500
millions period: 496
thousands period: 321
ones period: 784

11. ones period: 493
thousands period: 682
billions period: 578
millions period: 305

12. millions period: 249
thousands period: 638
billions period: 187
ones period: 541

_____   _____   _____

13. 500,000,000 + 60,000,000 + 3,000,000 + 100,000 + 70,000

_____

14. 8,000,000,000 + 40,000,000 + 6,000,000 + 300,000

_____

15. five hundred seventy-eight million, two hundred sixty-three thousand

_____

16. nine billion, three hundred fifty-one million, four hundred sixty-seven thousand

_____

Comparing and Ordering Whole Numbers

Write >, <, or = in each ◯.

1.　　652 ◯ 649　　　　　**2.**　5,672 ◯ 5,680　　　**3.**　7,988 ◯ 7,986

4.　23,465 ◯ 23,645　　**5.**　10,000 ◯ 9,999　　**6.**　632,097 ◯ 632,097

7.　785,039 ◯ 785,309　**8.**　5,678 ◯ 5,867　　**9.**　3,050 ◯ 3,005

10.　40 thousand ◯ 4,900　　　　　**11.**　823 thousand ◯ 832,000

12.　37 million ◯ 37,000,000　　　**13.**　65 billion ◯ 905,000,000

Write the numbers in order from greatest to least.

14.　6,489　6,491　6,487　6,495　　　**15.**　78,564　78,654　78,465

_____　　　_____

16.　986　1,009　989　968　　　　　**17.**　435,900　436,900　456,900

_____　　　_____

Write the numbers from the box that are:

18.　greater than 376,613 _____

19.　less than 55,000 _____

20.　between 250,000 and 340,000 _____

21.　greater than 38,000 and less than 63,000 _____

22.　between 45,000 and 200,000 _____

| 68,725 |
| 656,456 |
| 357,979 |
| 56,784 |
| 323,498 |
| 19,107 |
| 43,192 |
| 283,217 |
| 24,589 |
| 398,004 |
| 172,830 |
| 235,482 |

Rounding Whole Numbers

Round to the nearest ten.

1. 275 _____ **2.** 462 _____ **3.** 586 _____

4. 3,144 _____ **5.** 8,633 _____ **6.** 4,286 _____

Round to the nearest hundred.

7. 465 _____ **8.** 6,130 _____ **9.** 3,642 _____

10. 2,451 _____ **11.** 4,890 _____ **12.** 10,135 _____

13. 14,587 _____ **14.** 26,483 _____ **15.** 42,050 _____

16. 6,452 _____ **17.** 210 _____ **18.** 22,361 _____

Round to the nearest thousand.

19. 4,631 _____ **20.** 2,503 _____ **21.** 7,821 _____

22. 21,965 _____ **23.** 16,489 _____ **24.** 40,634 _____

25. 8,099 _____ **26.** 34,530 _____ **27.** 18,000 _____

Round to the nearest ten thousand.

28. 373,456 _____ **29.** 785,692 _____ **30.** 250,416 _____

31. 919,622 _____ **32.** 462,460 _____ **33.** 379,907 _____

34. 558,285 _____ **35.** 247,003 _____ **36.** 999,534 _____

Round each number to the greatest possible place, the place farthest left.

37. 9,846 _____ **38.** 35,468 _____

39. 20,243,310 _____ **40.** 110,479 _____

41. 985,679,452 _____ **42.** 1,865,971 _____

Name _____

Draw a Picture

Use the following information to finish drawing and labeling the picture. Then use the picture to help you solve the problems.

0   3   18
Danforth Burnham   Tuxedo

Donna, Butch, and Harry entered the Tuxedo Bike-athon. Donna rode the entire 18-mile course from Danforth to Tuxedo. Butch started at Burnham, 3 miles from Danforth. He stopped at Starlight. Butch rode $\frac{1}{2}$ as far as Donna. Harry started at Danforth and ended at Tribble, 3 miles past Burnham.

1. How far did Butch ride? _____

2. How far did Harry ride? _____

How far is it from:

3. Danforth to Tuxedo?   _____

4. Danforth to Starlight?   _____

5. Danforth to Tribble?   _____

6. Tribble to Starlight?   _____

7. Tribble to Tuxedo?   _____

8. Starlight to Tuxedo?   _____

Exploring Algebra: Variables and Expressions

Find the value of each expression when $n = 5$.

1. $n + 6 =$ _____

2. $n - 3 =$ _____

3. $n \times 1 =$ _____

4. $n \times n =$ _____

5. $n - 5 =$ _____

6. $20 \div n =$ _____

7. $2 \times n =$ _____

8. $16 + n =$ _____

9. $n + 10 =$ _____

10. $n \times 0 =$ _____

Find the value of each expression when $y = 18$.

11. $y + 0 =$ _____

12. $1 \times y =$ _____

13. $y \div 3 =$ _____

14. $y \div 6 =$ _____

15. $y + 9 =$ _____

16. $y \div 18 =$ _____

17. $2 \times y =$ _____

18. $20 + y =$ _____

19. $27 - y =$ _____

20. $30 - y =$ _____

Find the value of each expression when $b = 25$.

21. $4 \times b =$ _____

22. $b \times 1 =$ _____

23. $75 - b =$ _____

24. $b - 0 =$ _____

25. $b + b =$ _____

26. $50 - b =$ _____

27. $100 \div b =$ _____

28. $18 + b =$ _____

29. $0 \times b =$ _____

30. $100 - b =$ _____

Decimal Place Value: Tenths and Hundredths

Write the decimal place for each picture.

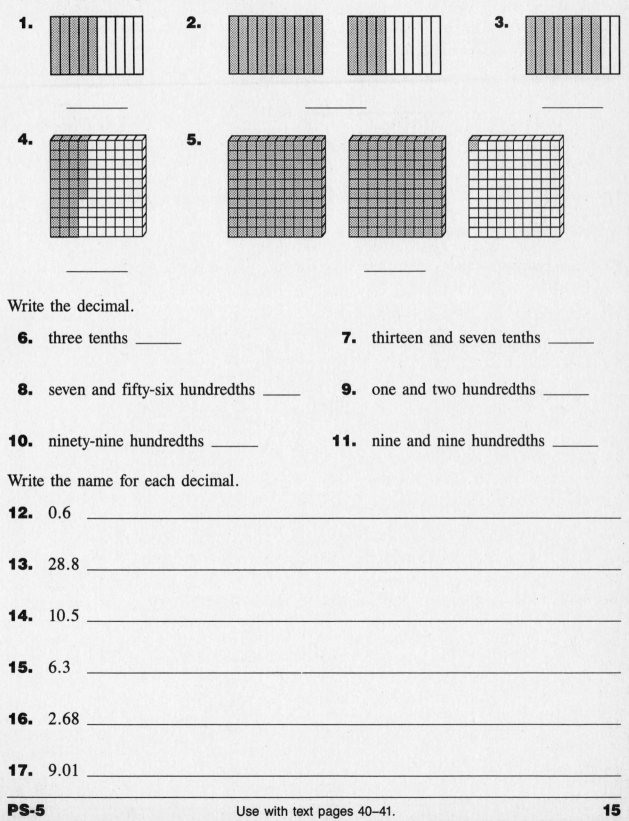

1.

2.

3.

_____   _____   _____

4.

5.

_____   _____

Write the decimal.

6. three tenths _____

7. thirteen and seven tenths _____

8. seven and fifty-six hundredths _____

9. one and two hundredths _____

10. ninety-nine hundredths _____

11. nine and nine hundredths _____

Write the name for each decimal.

12. 0.6 _____

13. 28.8 _____

14. 10.5 _____

15. 6.3 _____

16. 2.68 _____

17. 9.01 _____

Thousandths

Write the place-value of the 4 in each decimal.

1. 6.324 _____ **2.** 14.720 _____ **3.** 18.341 _____

4. 4.631 _____ **5.** 19.542 _____ **6.** 0.465 _____

Write the place-value name of the 9 in each decimal.

7. 39.481 _____ **8.** 0.769 _____ **9.** 2.896 _____

10. 1.395 _____ **11.** 7.249 _____ **12.** 10.954 _____

Write each number in standard form.

13. two and three hundred sixty-four thousandths _____

14. nine hundred twenty-five thousandths _____

15. four and sixteen hundredths _____

16. nineteen and twenty-three thousandths _____

17. eighty-one thousandths _____

18. twenty-seven and forty-three hundredths _____

19. two hundred sixty-four and seven tenths _____

20. fifty-three and six thousandths _____

Write the word name for each decimal.

21. 5.031 _____

22. 4.628 _____

23. 0.905 _____

Comparing and Ordering Decimals

Write $<$, $>$, or $=$ in each $\bigcirc$.

1. 0.467 $\bigcirc$ 0.465   **2.**   3.5 $\bigcirc$ 3.50   **3.** 4.07 $\bigcirc$ 4.70

4.   2.06 $\bigcirc$ 2.3   **5.**   0.61 $\bigcirc$ 0.59   **6.** 0.49 $\bigcirc$ 0.9

7.   38.4 $\bigcirc$ 3.84   **8.**   7 $\bigcirc$ 6.98   **9.**   2.7 $\bigcirc$ 2.69

10. 0.320 $\bigcirc$ 0.32   **11.**   0.99 $\bigcirc$ 1.00   **12.**   9.8 $\bigcirc$ 8.9

13.   2.1 $\bigcirc$ 21   **14.** 0.386 $\bigcirc$ 0.368   **15.** 1.01 $\bigcirc$ 0.99

Write the number or numbers from the box that are:

16. less than 0.025 _____

17. greater than 3.5 _____

0.04	3.507
0.012	3.45
3.72	2.98
0.25	1.10
0.027	2.46
2.55	0.02

18. greater than 0.125 and less than 1.125 _____

19. between 2.5 and 3 _____

List the decimals from the box
in order from greatest to least.

20.

0.559	0.601
0.441	0.438

21.

0.324	0.328
0.342	0.336

_____   _____

Rounding Decimals

Round to the nearest whole number.

1. 5.2 _____   **2.** 6.7 _____   **3.** 4.5 _____

4. 1.3 _____   **5.** 4.36 _____   **6.** 3.081 _____

7. 9.91 _____   **8.** 0.69 _____   **9.** 3.02 _____

10. 28.40 _____   **11.** 17.83 _____   **12.** 0.82 _____

13. 14.4 _____   **14.** 29.5 _____   **15.** 1.613 _____

Round to the nearest tenth.

16. 0.63 _____   **17.** 0.18 _____   **18.** 3.62 _____

19. 2.811 _____   **20.** 5.036 _____   **21.** 0.45 _____

22. 1.49 _____   **23.** 8.849 _____   **24.** 2.05 _____

25. 9.049 _____   **26.** 0.95 _____   **27.** 0.961 _____

28. 4.38 _____   **29.** 6.109 _____   **30.** 1.255 _____

Round to the nearest hundredth.

31. 2.736 _____   **32.** 0.864 _____   **33.** 6.493 _____

34. 4.675 _____   **35.** 8.129 _____   **36.** 3.798 _____

37. 0.546 _____   **38.** 25.683 _____   **39.** 17.291 _____

40. 34.671 _____   **41.** 5.696 _____   **42.** 8.545 _____

Name _____

Understanding the Question

Ask the question another way. Then use any strategy to solve.

1. The Tasty Tea Company produced 6,792 tea bags one day. If they put 24 tea bags in each box, how many boxes do they need?

_____

2. A carton of tea bags contains 12 boxes. If there are 24 tea bags in a box, how many are there in a carton?

_____

3. One truck has 854 cartons of tea to deliver. Another has 783 cartons. How many cartons are to be delivered in all?

_____

4. One day the Tasty Tea Company boxed 524 boxes of cinnamon tea and 329 boxes of lemon tea. How many more boxes of cinnamon tea were there?

_____

Solve.

5. There are 2,772 boxes of tea ready to be put in cartons. If there are 12 boxes in a carton, how many cartons are needed?

_____

6. There are 1,524 cartons of tea in the warehouse. If the Tasty Tea Company fills an order for 700 cartons of tea, how many cartons will be left?

_____

7. 12 stores ordered a total of 6,300 boxes of tea. If each store ordered the same number of boxes, how many boxes does each receive?

_____

8. Each Tasty Tea delivery truck can hold 948 cartons of tea. How many cartons can 8 trucks hold?

_____

9. Two delivery trucks were 1,000 miles apart. To meet, each truck drove 300 miles toward the other. How far apart were the two trucks then?

_____

10. A Tasty Tea delivery truck made a trip to a city 130 miles away. If it returned by the same route, how far did it travel in all?

_____

Name _____

Using Rounding

Estimate by rounding so that you can use mental math.

1.	463 − 250	**2.**	8.9 + 2.7	**3.**	$6.39 − 1.65	**4.**	638 + 410

5.	$8.14 + 7.79	**6.**	698 − 452	**7.**	1,781 − 945	**8.**	$9.50 + 3.79

9.	$5.29 − 2.43	**10.**	17,498 − 8,329	**11.**	145 + 78	**12.**	124 − 66

13.	7.2 + 3.3	**14.**	$43.85 + 10.06	**15.**	65.4 − 64.3	**16.**	16.4 − 11.8

17.	12,645 − 9,103	**18.**	4,289 + 8,500	**19.**	$5.25 + 4.49

20.	5,392 + 7,100	**21.**	1,014 + 5,421	**22.**	9,801 − 2,381

23.	$6.98 + 5.62	**24.**	5,905 − 2,761	**25.**	4,257 − 2,804

Name _____

Reviewing Whole Number Addition and Subtraction

Add or subtract.

1.
$$\begin{array}{r} 93 \\ + 84 \\ \hline \end{array}$$

2.
$$\begin{array}{r} 46 \\ + 32 \\ \hline \end{array}$$

3.
$$\begin{array}{r} 75 \\ - 17 \\ \hline \end{array}$$

4.
$$\begin{array}{r} 44 \\ - 29 \\ \hline \end{array}$$

5.
$$\begin{array}{r} 268 \\ - 39 \\ \hline \end{array}$$

6.
$$\begin{array}{r} 471 \\ - 89 \\ \hline \end{array}$$

7.
$$\begin{array}{r} 363 \\ + 175 \\ \hline \end{array}$$

8.
$$\begin{array}{r} 725 \\ + 503 \\ \hline \end{array}$$

9.
$$\begin{array}{r} 865 \\ - 557 \\ \hline \end{array}$$

10.
$$\begin{array}{r} 367 \\ - 244 \\ \hline \end{array}$$

11.
$$\begin{array}{r} 746 \\ + 185 \\ \hline \end{array}$$

12.
$$\begin{array}{r} 609 \\ + 893 \\ \hline \end{array}$$

13.
$$\begin{array}{r} 43,689 \\ + 26,603 \\ \hline \end{array}$$

14.
$$\begin{array}{r} 37,765 \\ + 11,485 \\ \hline \end{array}$$

15.
$$\begin{array}{r} 44,568 \\ - 32,179 \\ \hline \end{array}$$

16.
$$\begin{array}{r} 26,447 \\ - 12,768 \\ \hline \end{array}$$

17.
$$\begin{array}{r} 3,645 \\ 9,385 \\ + \quad 27 \\ \hline \end{array}$$

18.
$$\begin{array}{r} 1,093 \\ 7,884 \\ + 1,534 \\ \hline \end{array}$$

19.
$$\begin{array}{r} 62,301 \\ - 13,269 \\ \hline \end{array}$$

20.
$$\begin{array}{r} 23,008 \\ - 1,741 \\ \hline \end{array}$$

21. $3,437 + 465$

22. $12,465 + 7,655$

23. $9,874 - 8,887$

24. $67,322 - 42,741$

Front-End Estimation

Use front-end digits to estimate. Then use a
calculator to tell whether the exact sum or
difference is more or less than your estimate.

1.	483 + 421	**2.**	552 − 360	**3.**	173 + 829

4.	966 − 741	**5.**	525 + 79	**6.**	610 − 221

7.	398 + 709	**8.**	848 − 455	**9.**	872 304 + 235

10.	168 340 + 597	**11.**	487 395 + 683	**12.**	751 348 + 819

13.	$3.42 + 4.63	**14.**	$9.58 − 6.49	**15.**	$5.98 + 5.79

16.	$7.15 − 3.24	**17.**	329 + 649	**18.**	850 − 103

19.	615 + 592	**20.**	487 + 826	**21.**	563 + 491

22.	912 − 768	**23.**	785 − 131	**24.**	118 + 772

Guess and Check

Use the strategy Guess and Check to help you solve each problem.

1. Toby rode the train 10 more times than Bill did. Altogether both boys rode the train 60 times. How many times did Bill ride?

_____

2. A movie ticket and popcorn cost $5. The ticket costs 4 times as much as the popcorn. How much does popcorn cost?

_____

3. Eric and Albert won prizes for selling the most raffle tickets for the Spring Fling. Together they sold 100 tickets. Albert sold 16 tickets more than Eric. How many did each sell?

_____

4. Sue and Bob both jumped rope to raise money for new gym equipment. Together they earned $24. Sue earned twice as much as Bob. How much money did each earn?

_____

5. Emil had great luck at the Go-Fish game, but Kim did not. Together they won 16 prizes. Emi won 10 more than Kim. How many did each win?

_____

6. There were 20 more fifth graders at the fair than there were fourth graders. 140 students from both grades came. How many fifth graders came to the fair?

_____

7. Shirley and Amy painted faces at the fair for an hour. Sixteen children had their faces painted. Shirley was able to paint 3 times as many faces as Amy. How many faces did each girl paint?

_____

8. The school has raised $1,200 over the last 2 years at the Spring Fling. This year the school raised $200 more than last year. How much money did the school raise at the fair last year?

_____

Adding Decimals: Making the Connection

Use place value blocks to solve. Record your work
using symbols.

1. 3.45 + 1.75 = _____   **2.** 6.96 + 1.15 = _____

3. 6.2 + 0.84 = _____   **4.** 7.82 + 2.1 = _____

5. 4.16 + 1.73 = _____   **6.** 2.83 + 0.67 = _____

7. 1.18 + 1.82 = _____   **8.** 3.31 + 4.71 = _____

9. 4.43 + 0.56 = _____   **10.** 5.46 + 3.41 = _____

Use place value blocks to add. Record your work
using symbols.

11. 0.32   **12.** 5.16   **13.** 2.46
      + 0.84   + 3.32   + 3.54

14. 4.19   **15.** 0.76   **16.** 7.03
      + 2.81   + 0.25   + 1.28

17. 3.26   **18.** 5.04   **19.** 3.69
      + 1.75   + 2.97   + 2.47

20. What must be added to 0.37 to get 1?
        Use blocks to show that your answer is correct.

        _____

Name _____

Adding Decimals

Add.

1.   0.6
       + 0.8

2.   17.6
      + 6.3

3.   0.68
     + 6.73

4.   8.95
     + 1.37

5. $6.64
    + 0.98

6. $3.84
    + 5.78

7. $5.64
    + 7.57

8.   0.326
    + 0.487

9.   62.5
    + 49.7

10.   28.65
   + 93.71

11.   84.58
   + 9.73

12.   76.57
   + 32.8

13. 402.4 + 0.9 + 54.54   **14.** 7.6 + 63.07 + 0.44   **15.** 48.54 + 3.6 + 383.001

Use rounding to the place of the underlined digit to estimate each sum.

16. $\underline{5}.6 + \underline{8}.3$ **17.** $\underline{4}9.8 + \underline{5}0.01$ **18.** $\$\underline{7}.45 + \$\underline{3}.92$

Using Critical Thinking

Suppose each set of cards was produced by a function machine. Give the function rule for each.

1.

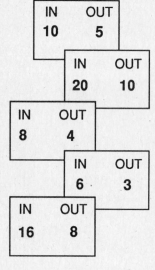

IN	OUT
10	5
20	10
8	4
6	3
16	8

Rule: _____

_____

2.

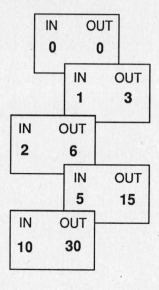

IN	OUT
0	0
1	3
2	6
5	15
10	30

Rule: _____

_____

3.

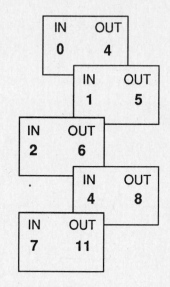

IN	OUT
0	4
1	5
2	6
4	8
7	11

Rule: _____

_____

4.

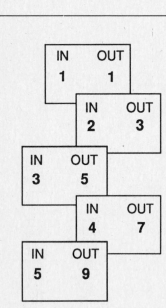

IN	OUT
1	1
2	3
3	5
4	7
5	9

Rule: _____

_____

_____

5.

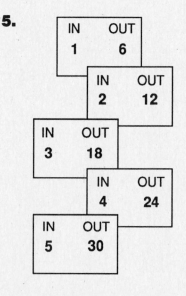

IN	OUT
1	6
2	12
3	18
4	24
5	30

Rule: _____

_____

_____

6.

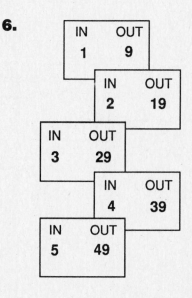

IN	OUT
1	9
2	19
3	29
4	39
5	49

Rule: _____

_____

_____

Choosing a Calculation Method

	Soup & Sandwich Shop Homemade Soups & Breads		
Soups	*Sandwiches*	*Drinks*	
Fresh vegetable $0.75	Egg salad $1.24	Juice small	$0.29
Chicken noodle 0.87	Tuna salad 1.45	medium	0.49
Split pea w/ham 0.98	Roast beef 1.84	large	0.69
Chili 1.29	Ham 1.78	Milk medium	0.39
		large	0.59

Lunch Special $2.50
(Soup, Salad, Sandwich, Milk)

Solve. Choose an appropriate calculation method.

1. Today 6 people are each having the lunch special. How much will their lunches cost in all?

2. If the shop sells 336 roast beef sandwiches a week, how many will it sell in a year (52 weeks)?

3. Which lunch costs more, a bowl of chili and a ham sandwich or a bowl of vegetable soup and a roast beef sandwich? How much more?

4. Each person in a group of 4 is having chili, a tuna salad sandwich, and a medium juice. How much will their order cost in all?

5. Andrew has $5. How much will he have left if he buys a bowl of vegetable soup, an egg salad sandwich, and a large milk?

6. How much more does a bowl of chicken noodle soup, a ham sandwich, and a large juice cost than a lunch special?

Subtracting Decimals: Making the Connection

Show how you use place value blocks to subtract.
Record the trades and how many are left in the chart.
Write the difference as a decimal.

Example: 4.12
            − 3.91
            ‾‾‾‾‾‾
             0.21

	3	11	2
−	3	9	1
	0	2	1

---

1.   3.84
        − 2.68

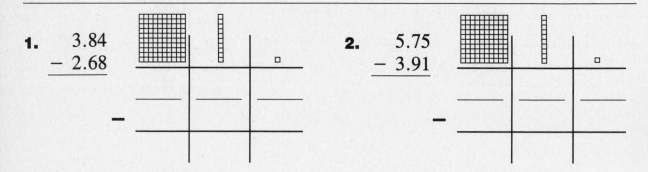

2.   5.75
        − 3.91

3.   2.48
        − 1.96

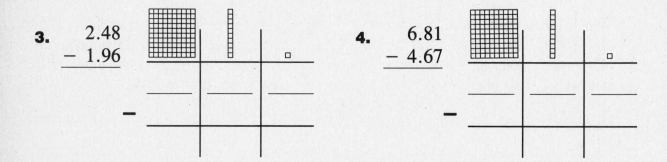

4.   6.81
        − 4.67

5.   4.23
        − 2.18

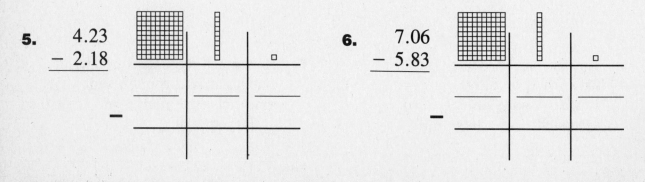

6.   7.06
        − 5.83

Subtracting Decimals

Subtract.

1.   3.2
    − 0.9

2.   15.7
    − 8.9

3.   7.032
    − 5.926

4.   8.75
    − 2.39

5.   5.82
    − 1.65

6.   6.504
    − 3.688

7.   0.871
    − 0.682

8.   4.93
    − 0.99

9.   132.6
    − 106.7

10.   5.90
    − 2.94

11.   582.731
    − 236.695

12.   30.17
    − 18.92

13. $10.61
    −   1.96

14. $52.81
    − 22.09

15. $672.14
    − 181.12

16. $803.42
    −   95.17

17. 15.1 − 8.6

15.1
− 8.6

18. 4.160 − 0.374

4.160
− 0.374

19. 3,108.1 − 659.3

3,108.1
− 659.3

Use rounding to estimate each difference to the place
value of the underlined digit.

20. 159.63 − 19.82

21. $16.07 − $8.53

22. 17.6 − 8.3

Using Compensation

Find the exact sums and differences mentally. Use compensation.

1. 53 + 47 _____

2. 98 + 16 _____

3. 39 + 45 _____

4. 83 + 19 _____

5. 46 − 29 _____

6. 32 − 21 _____

7. 51 − 26 _____

8. 63 − 49 _____

9. 498 + 62 _____

10. 168 + 295 _____

11. 597 + 403 _____

12. 997 + 136 _____

13. 556 − 199 _____

15. 487 − 303 _____

14. 556 + 199 _____

16. 487 + 303 _____

17. 611 − 599 _____

19. 413 − 298 _____

18. 611 + 599 _____

20. 413 + 298 _____

21. 56 − 49 _____

23. 102 − 75 _____

22. 56 + 49 _____

24. 102 + 75 _____

Using a Calculator

Use any problem-solving strategy to solve. Write *C*
if you used your calculator's constant feature.

1. The 23-member track team needs new warm-up suits. Parents will donate $4 toward each suit. How much will parents donate?

_____

2. Shelly and Raymond Jackson together spent $82 on new equipment. Shelly spent 26 more than her brother. How much did each spend?

_____

3. The track team is considering four suits, each listed at a different price. Fill in the chart below to compare the total costs for 23 suits.

Suit	Unit Price	Total Cost
Comfort Zone	$25	
Sun Sport	$28	
Go for Gold	$29	
Speed Test	$39	

4. Family memberships cost $126 more than single memberships for each program at the community center. Complete the chart to show family membership costs.

Program	Single Membership	Family Membership
All facilities	$207	
Swim and gym	$186	
Tennis and gym	$152	

5. Altogether $216 was raised toward the total cost of the suits. Use the total costs calculated in Problem 3 and record the balance the team would owe for each type of suit.

Suit	Team Cost
Comfort Zone	
Sun Sport	
Go for Gold	
Speed Test	

6. Nineteen team members ordered time watches. The total cost was $380. How much did each watch cost?

_____

7. Kiran's favorite running shoe regularly costs $68. She was able to buy it for $46. How much did she save?

_____

Thinking About Graphs

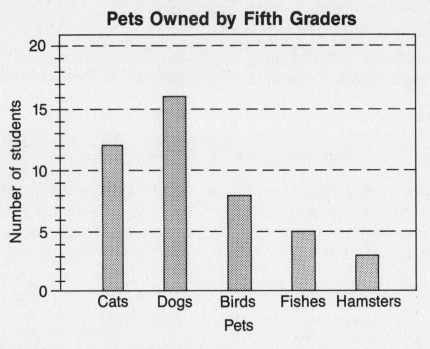

Pets Owned by Fifth Graders

Use the bar graph to answer each question.

1. What is the title of the bar graph?

_____

_____

2. What are the labels for the sides of the bar graph?

_____

_____

3. What pet is owned by the most students?

_____

4. What pet is owned by the fewest students?

_____

Use the pictograph to answer the questions.

Fifth Graders on Sports Teams

Baseball 🧍🧍🧍🧍
Soccer   🧍🧍🧍
Basketball 🧍🧍
Tennis   🧍🧍

🧍 = 10 students   🧍 = 5 students

5. What is the title of the pictograph?

_____

6. What is the key for the pictograph?

_____

_____

Reading and Interpreting Line Graphs

Bicycle Sales for One Year

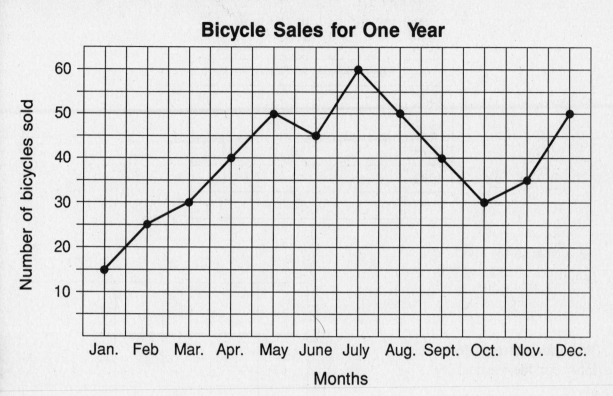

Use the line graph to answer each question.

1. How many bicycles were sold in January?

_____

2. During which month were the same number of bicycles sold as were sold in April?

_____

3. How many bicycles were sold in March?

_____

4. During which months were fewer than 30 bicycles sold?

_____

5. In which month were the most bicycles sold?

_____

6. Did the number of bicycles sales increase or decrease from May to June?

_____

7. How many bicycles were sold in December?

_____

8. During which months were more than 45 bicycles sold?

_____

Making Line Graphs

Complete the line graph below using the data in the table.

Year	Trees Planted in Scrabble Park
1986	6
1987	18
1988	15
1989	9
1990	12

1. Write a title for the graph.

2. Write an appropriate label for the vertical scale.

3. Write an appropriate label for the horizontal side of the graph.

4. Plot and connect the points for the graph.

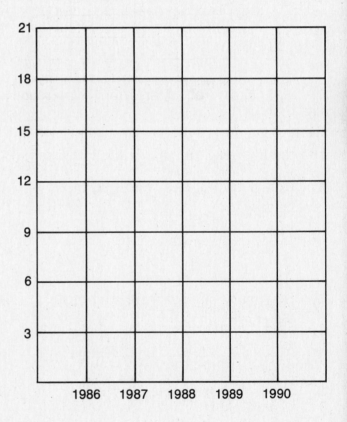

Answer each question.

5. In which year were the fewest trees planted?

_____

6. In which year were the most trees planted?

_____

Name _____

Double Bar Graphs

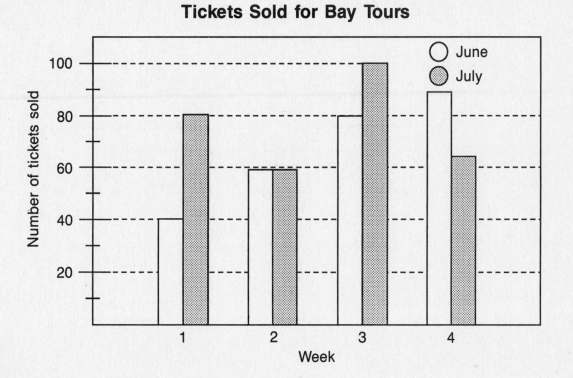

Tickets Sold for Bay Tours

Use the double bar graph to answer each question.

1. How many tickets were sold during the third week in June?

_____

2. During which week were the same number of tickets sold in June as in July?

_____

3. In which week during these months were the most tickets sold?

_____

4. During which week were twice as many tickets sold in July as in June?

_____

5. During which week were more tickets sold in June than in July?

_____

6. In which week during these months were the fewest tickets sold?

_____

7. How many tickets were sold during the fourth week in July?

_____

8. During which month were the most tickets sold for the third week?

_____

Using Critical Thinking

Use the graph to answer the questions.

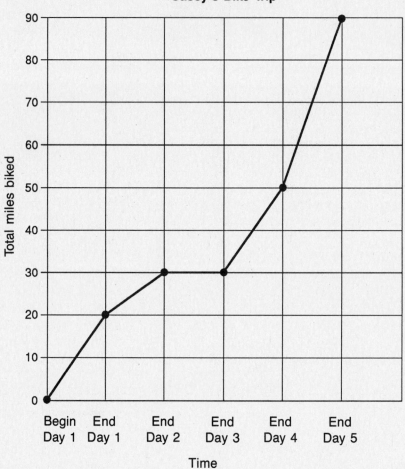

Casey's Bike Trip

1. What days did Casey bike the same

   distance? _____

   How far did he go? _____

2. Which day did Casey stay in Farmont and spend the whole day at the county fair? _____

3. What is the farthest distance

   Casey biked in one day? _____

4. What is the least distance Casey covered on the days that he

   biked? _____

5. How far did Casey bike on

   Days 4 and 5? _____

Running Totals with a Calculator

The drama club was taking a trip to the theater in
New York. the cost for each student was $220.
Sandra, Tony, and Kelly worked to earn the cost of
the trip. Their earnings each month are shown in
the table.

Earnings

	Sandra	Tony	Kelly
September	$78	$64	$36
October	$88	$58	$68
November	$46	$62	$54
December	$36	$38	$34
January	$38	$50	$52

Examine the data in the table. Use your calculator
to solve each problem.

1. When did each student reach the
$220 goal?

_____

_____

2. Which student earned the most?

_____

3. The students used extra earnings
as spending money. How much
spending money did each student earn?

_____

_____

4. If the cost of the trip had been
$150, when would each student have
reached the goal?

_____

_____

Range, Mean, Median, and Mode

Find the range, mean, median, and mode for each set
of data. Fill in the chart.

	Range	Mean	Median	Mode
1				
2				
3				
4				
5				
6				

1. 225, 275, 190, 211, 263, 259, 205, 204

2. $20.00, $14.00, $24.75, $15.75, $22.50, $17.50, $13.25

3. 81, 87, 91, 94, 97, 71, 83, 87, 92

4. 63, 67, 43, 40, 51, 78, 89, 89

5. 103, 113, 107, 104, 103

6. 24, 15, 20, 30, 52, 45

Making a Questionnaire

Fifth-Grade Survey
How Do You Spend Your Time After School?
1. What grade are you in?   K-2   3-5   6-8
2. Do you have sports practice after school?   Yes   No
3. How much television do you watch a day?   1 hour   2 hours   3 hours
4. How much allowance do you get per week? $0-$2 $2-$4 $4-$10

Byron wants to find out how the students in his
fifth-grade class spend their time after school.
He has written some questions for the fifth graders,
but they need revision.

1. Why is Question 1 unnecessary? _____

_____

2. How could Byron rewrite Question 2 so that he would get more information? _____

_____

3. Why could some students have trouble answering Question 3? _____

_____

_____

4. Why is Question 4 confusing? _____

_____

5. Should Question 4 be on this questionnaire? _____

_____

Name _____

Make a Table

Complete the tables to solve the problems.

1. Out of every 11 people whom Sabrina asked to buy cookies, 7 people did. At this rate, how many people can she expect to buy cookies if she asks 44 people?

People asked	11			
Cookie buyers	7			

_____

2. Lauren sells popcorn at the movies. Out of every 9 people who come to the theater, 5 buy popcorn. If 45 people are expected at the next show, how many should she expect to buy popcorn?

Theater goers	9				
Popcorn buyers	5				

_____

3. Last summer at camp it rained 2 days out of every 5. At that rate, how many days should it rain this year if camp lasts 30 days?

Days	5					
Rainy days	2					

_____

4. William took a survey and found that 3 out of 5 students in his class ride the bus to school. If there are 25 students in William's class, how many can he expect to ride the bus to school?

Students	5				
Bus riders	3				

_____

Name _____

Substituting Compatible Numbers

Dog Supplies			
Dog collar	$5.69	Squeaky toy	$3.66
Dog leash	$10.19	Dog food	$5.49
Dog dish	$5.12	Dog shampoo	$4.78
Dog bones	$4.89	Dog brush	$3.54

Richard has a new dog. Substitute compatible numbers
to estimate the cost of supplies.

1. collar and leash _____

2. toy and bones _____

3. dish and food _____

4. food and bones _____

5. shampoo and brush _____

6. 2 dishes _____

Substitute compatible numbers to estimate each sum
or difference.

7. 268 − 54 _____

8. 274 + 145 _____

9. 574 + 396 _____

10. 229 + 170 _____

11. 505 − 295 _____

12. 480 − 231 _____

13. 879 − 441 _____

14. 559 + 299 _____

15. 654 + 74 _____

16. 437 − 181 _____

17. $533 + $254 + $999 + $248 _____

18. $673 + $120 + $345 + $166 _____

Name _____

Extra Data

Solve. Underline the extra data.

1. The students at Hunters Point School participate in the park cleanup each year. Last year 500 students and their families worked. This year 525 students and their families worked for 6 hours. How many more students and their families worked this year than last year?

_____

2. Mark's team had 16 members. The local television station spent 15 minutes filming them as they cleared debris from the stream. The film took 30 seconds on the evening news. At that rate, how long would it take the television crew to film a 60-second segment of news?

_____

3. Fran had to leave 2 hours early. There were 9 more people on her team who worked from 9 a.m. until 3 p.m. How many hours did Fran work?

_____

4. The fourth graders sold T-shirts that said "Keep Your Park Clean!" Each shirt cost $6.00. They sold twice as many small shirts as large ones. How many large shirts did they sell if they sold 42 small ones?

_____

5. The 75 fifth graders raised $150 to provide trash bags and other supplies. They can buy 30 bags for $3.00. About how much money did each fifth grader earn for the cleanup?

_____

6. The local supermarket donated 720 canned drinks and 500 bags of chips. If drinks come in packs of 6, how many were there?

_____

7. Two out of every 5 students at the cleanup brought a member of their family with them. There were twice as many parents as there were brothers or sisters. In a group of 25 students, how many family members were there?

_____

8. Three teams worked hauling away dead branches. Each team worked $1\frac{1}{2}$ hours. There were 8 people on each team. How many people worked hauling branches?

_____

Special Products

Multiply.

1. 90×90 = _____ **2.** 50×600 = _____

3. 50×50 = _____ **4.** 40×500 = _____

5. 70×500 = _____ **6.** 90×80 = _____

7. 10×30 = _____ **8.** 40×600 = _____

9. 80×50 = _____ **10.** 700×600 = _____

11. 400×700 = _____ **12.** 300×90 = _____

13. 90×70 = _____ **14.** 70×100 = _____

15. 50×80 = _____ **16.** 300×80 = _____

17. 50×300 = _____ **18.** 90×60 = _____

19. 40×90 = _____ **20.** 50×200 = _____

21. 800×30 = _____ **22.** 60×50 = _____

23. 70×40 = _____ **24.** 600×400 = _____

25. 50×90 = _____ **26.** 200×80 = _____

27. 50×900 = _____ **28.** 60×500 = _____

29. $70 \times 40 \times 10$ = _____ **30.** $10 \times 500 \times 80$ = _____

31. $40 \times 30 \times 20$ = _____ **32.** $80 \times 200 \times 40$ = _____

33. $10 \times 60 \times 90$ = _____ **34.** $80 \times 10 \times 80$ = _____

35. $70 \times 90 \times 100$ = _____ **36.** $20 \times 30 \times 60$ = _____

Estimating Products Using Rounding

Estimate by rounding.

1. 93 × 59 _____   **2.** 68 × 73 _____   **3.** 76 × 54 _____

4. 52 × 48 _____   **5.** 24 × 27 _____   **6.** 29 × 36 _____

7. 13 × 97 _____   **8.** 42 × 83 _____   **9.** 69 × 71 _____

10. 9 × 64 _____   **11.** 12 × 22 _____   **12.** 65 × 53 _____

13. 592 × 41 _____   **14.** 734 × 68 _____   **15.** 486 × 83 _____

16. 210 × 57 _____   **17.** 397 × 29 _____   **18.** 832 × 52 _____

19. 105 × 28 _____   **20.** 672 × 16 _____   **21.** 915 × 77 _____

22. 531 × 19 _____   **23.** 402 × 56 _____   **24.** 275 × 98 _____

Use estimation to find two factor pairs from the list whose product is close to:

25. 3,600 _____

26. 1,600 _____

27. 2,000 _____

28. 6,000 _____

29. 4,000 _____

30. 2,100 _____

31. 2,400 _____

32. 4,500 _____

37 × 89	18 × 78
61 × 101	62 × 39
37 × 41	48 × 81
53 × 86	23 × 98
62 × 98	47 × 92
29 × 72	41 × 97
58 × 62	42 × 52
28 × 83	33 × 68

Name _____

Reviewing Whole Number Multiplication

Multiply.

1.	47 $\times\ 7$	**2.**	285 $\times\ \ 4$	**3.**	4,725 $\times\ \ \ \ 6$	**4.**	3,192 $\times\ \ \ \ 9$

5.	27 $\times\ 79$	**6.**	40 $\times\ 80$	**7.**	12 $\times\ 85$	**8.**	42 $\times\ 74$

9.	409 $\times\ \ 63$	**10.**	624 $\times\ \ 83$	**11.**	367 $\times\ \ 41$	**12.**	176 $\times\ \ 13$

13.	600 $\times\ \ 80$	**14.**	273 $\times\ \ 21$	**15.**	928 $\times\ \ 77$	**16.**	564 $\times\ \ 60$

Multiple-Step Problems

Solve. Use any problem-solving strategy.

1. Elmer paid $25 for a day pack and $38 for a cook stove. What was the total bill if the tax was $4?

_____

2. The hiking club bought 32 books about hiking and 16 books about rock climbing. If each book costs $8, how much did they pay for the books?

_____

3. Roberta paid $4 for a campsite and $2 for firewood. She paid with a $10 bill. How much change did she receive?

_____

4. Wendy wants to buy a $12 flashlight, an $18 compass, and an $18 pedometer. If she saves $8 a week, how many weeks will it take to save enough money?

_____

5. One group of hikers took Fern Trail for 16 km and then took Canyon Trail. Their total hike was 28 km. Another group took Canyon Trail and then took Waterfall Trail for 6 km. How far did they hike?

_____

6. River Trail is 14 km long. Waterfall Trail is 6 km long. Mike took both trails. If he takes the same route back to camp, what will be the total distance he hikes?

_____

7. Art wants to buy a $285 tent. He has $45. If he saves $10 a week, how many weeks will it be before he can buy the tent?

_____

8. Travel expenses for a hiking trip were $80. Supplies cost $200. If 7 people went on the trip, how much did each person have to pay?

_____

Solve a Simpler Problem

1. Tiffany needs to get 36 one-inch strips from a piece of material that is one yard long. How many cuts will she have to make? _____

36 strips ⟶

2. Juan swims at the school pool. Different lanes are marked off for the swim team and for lap swimmers. Altogether there are 16 lanes. How many lane dividers are needed? _____

16 lanes ⟶

3. Spencer baked a pan of brownies. He made one long cut down the center of the pan and then made five cuts side to side. how many brownies did he get? _____

4. Rahji helped arrange tables in the art room. One table seats 4 students. How many tables did he push together end to end to create a cluster that would seat 12 students? _____

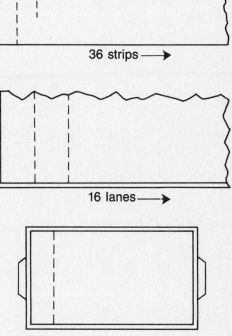

One table

Tables placed end to end

5. Larger tables were used for the Promotion Day Banquet. One of these tables seats 6. How many people can be seated if 8 tables are placed side by side? _____ How many people could be seated if 20 tables were placed together side by side? _____

One table

Tables placed side by side

6. What if the larger tables were placed end to end rather than side by side? How many people could be seated at 8 tables? _____ How many people could be seated at 20 tables? _____

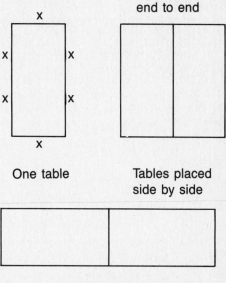

Tables placed end to end

Breaking Apart Numbers

Show how to use the distributive property to find
the products using mental math.

1. $4 \times 12 = (4 \times 10) + (4 \times 2) = $ _____

2. $5 \times 26 = (5 \times 20) + (5 \times 6) = $ _____

3. $3 \times 36 = ($ _____ $\times 30) + ($ _____ $\times 6) = $ _____

4. $6 \times 15 = (6 \times $ _____ $) + (6 \times 5) = $ _____

5. $4 \times 32 = (4 \times $ _____ $) + (4 \times $ _____ $) = $ _____

6. $7 \times 21 = (7 \times $ _____ $) + (7 \times $ _____ $) = $ _____

7. $2 \times 65 = (2 \times $ _____ $) + (2 \times $ _____ $) = $ _____

8. $9 \times 18 = ($ _____ $\times $ _____ $) + ($ _____ $\times $ _____ $) = $ _____

9. $5 \times 51 = ($ _____ $\times $ _____ $) + ($ _____ $\times $ _____ $) = $ _____

10. $8 \times 12 = ($ _____ $\times $ _____ $) + ($ _____ $\times $ _____ $) = $ _____

Use the distributive property and mental math to
find the products.

11. $9 \times 11 = $ _____   **12.** $5 \times 32 = $ _____

13. $6 \times 25 = $ _____   **14.** $9 \times 13 = $ _____

15. $5 \times 14 = $ _____   **16.** $3 \times 27 = $ _____

17. $2 \times 36 = $ _____   **18.** $2 \times 93 = $ _____

19. $7 \times 23 = $ _____   **20.** $4 \times 15 = $ _____

21. $6 \times 81 = $ _____   **22.** $7 \times 18 = $ _____

Multiplying Decimals: Making the Connection

Show each product on the grid. Write your
answer as a decimal.

1. 0.6×0.5

_____

2. 0.8×0.3

_____

3. 0.3×0.4

_____

4. 0.8×0.7

_____

5. 0.9×0.9

_____

6. 0.5×0.4

_____

7. 0.5×0.7

_____

8. 0.3×0.6

_____

Multiplying Decimals

Multiply.

1.　　5.3
　　× 0.5

2.　　3.51
　　× 0.4

3.　　0.68
　　×　5

4.　　2.15
　　×　6

5.　　5.2
　　× 1.6

6.　　0.35
　　× 4.2

7.　　1.08
　　× 26

8.　　8.3
　　× 0.52

9. 18 × 0.03

10. 2.07 × 5

11. 3.68 × 0.4

Copy the product. Write the decimal point in the correct place.

12.　　37.4
　　× 2.5
　　9350

13.　　0.5
　　× 0.7
　　035

14.　　2.4
　　× 0.3
　　072

15.　　3.9
　　× 0.01
　　0039

16. Find the product of 3.06 and 2.7.

17. If the factors are 4.7 and 12, what is the correct product?

Estimating with Decimals

Estimate your product. Use any estimation technique
you choose.

1. 5.37×6.62 _____   **2.** 2.86×5.03 _____   **3.** 7.12×0.884 _____

4. 3.71×4.32 _____   **5.** 7.8×3.22 _____   **6.** 6×2.04 _____

7. 30.45×59.16 _____   **8.** 621×1.93 _____   **9.** 6.83×81.8 _____

Estimate each sum. Use clustering.

10. $26.7 + 24.02 + 27.4 + 23.9$ _____

11. $97.83 + 105 + 94.6 + 110 + 92.2$ _____

12. $36.014 + 27.4 + 31.18$ _____

13. $46.8 + 56 + 49.17 + 47.8 + 53.04 + 45.6$ _____

14. $\$69.51 + \$75.00 + \$70.12$ _____

15. $\$889.12 + \$963.55 + \$1200.68 + \$952.89$ _____

16. $55.9 + 61.5 + 59.2 + 58.3 + 60.2$ _____

17. $79.82 + 83.056 + 80 + 77.52 + 84.072 + 82.3$ _____

18. $11.25 + 8.666 + 9.97 + 12 + 10.625$ _____

19. $160 + 224 + 210 + 189.32 + 175 + 206$ _____

20. $\$296.72 + \$275.25 + \$310.00 + \$268.42$ _____

More About Multiplying Decimals

Multiply. Write in zeros when necessary.

1.
$$\begin{array}{r} 0.04 \\ \times\ 0.9 \\ \hline \end{array}$$

2.
$$\begin{array}{r} 3.8 \\ \times\ 0.05 \\ \hline \end{array}$$

3.
$$\begin{array}{r} 0.7 \\ \times\ 0.02 \\ \hline \end{array}$$

4.
$$\begin{array}{r} 0.25 \\ \times\ 0.4 \\ \hline \end{array}$$

5.
$$\begin{array}{r} 5.3 \\ \times\ 0.08 \\ \hline \end{array}$$

6.
$$\begin{array}{r} 6.1 \\ \times\ 0.03 \\ \hline \end{array}$$

7.
$$\begin{array}{r} 0.88 \\ \times\ 0.7 \\ \hline \end{array}$$

8.
$$\begin{array}{r} 0.06 \\ \times\ 0.8 \\ \hline \end{array}$$

9.
$$\begin{array}{r} 568 \\ \times\ 0.005 \\ \hline \end{array}$$

10.
$$\begin{array}{r} 0.97 \\ \times\ 20 \\ \hline \end{array}$$

11.
$$\begin{array}{r} 70 \\ \times\ 0.06 \\ \hline \end{array}$$

12.
$$\begin{array}{r} 0.004 \\ \times\ 9 \\ \hline \end{array}$$

13.
$$\begin{array}{r} 27.6 \\ \times\ 5.2 \\ \hline \end{array}$$

14.
$$\begin{array}{r} 0.019 \\ \times\ 1.8 \\ \hline \end{array}$$

15.
$$\begin{array}{r} 5.71 \\ \times\ 3.9 \\ \hline \end{array}$$

16.
$$\begin{array}{r} 64 \\ \times\ 0.015 \\ \hline \end{array}$$

17. 0.07×0.4

18. $0.5 \times 0.09 \times 4$

19. $0.037 \times 6 \times 0.2$

Using a Calculator

Solve each problem. Use the memory keys when helpful.

1. Find the amount you should enclose to pay for this order. Do not forget to include tax.

Item	How Many	Price Each	Total Price
Swim cap	4	$ 1.49	
Swim goggles	3	4.99	
Tote bag	2	10.19	
Swimsuit	1	19.89	
Total for Goods			
Tax (0.05 × Total)			
Postage			3.15
Amount Enclosed			

2. Mr. Ross ordered 6 shirts costing $27.90 each. If tax is 0.05 of the total for goods, and postage is $1.23, how much money should he enclose?

_____

3. The basketball team ordered 4 basketballs costing $19.98 each (tax included). They also ordered a pump for $3.32 (tax included). If postage is $2.28, how much money should they enclose?

_____

4. A pair of roller skates costs $35.15 (tax included) if ordered from a catalog. Postage is $6.48. The same skates cost $39.95 in a local store. How much do you save by buying from the local store?

_____

5. The skating club ordered 5 protective helmets for $12.80 each. Tax is 0.05 of the total for the goods. If postage is $4.40, how much money should they enclose?

_____

Multiplying Decimals by 10, 100, and 1,000

Use mental math to find these products.

1. 10 × 4.0 _____

100 × 4.0 _____

1,000 × 4.0 _____

2. 10 × 6.95 _____

100 × 6.95 _____

1,000 × 6.95 _____

3. 10 × 2.92 _____

100 × 2.92 _____

1,000 × 2.92 _____

4. 10 × 0.28 _____

100 × 0.28 _____

1,000 × 0.28 _____

5. 10 × 0.05 _____

100 × 0.05 _____

1,000 × 0.05 _____

6. 10 × 52.63 _____

100 × 52.63 _____

1,000 × 52.63 _____

7. 10 × 16.5 _____

100 × 16.5 _____

1,000 × 16.5 _____

8. 10 × 436.75 _____

100 × 436.75 _____

1,000 × 436.75 _____

Use mental math to find the missing factors.

9. _____ 58.92 = 5,892

10. 0.0592 × _____ = 59.2

11. _____ × 6.3405 = 6,340.5

12. _____ × 3.1416 = 314.16

13. 383 × _____ = 38,300

14. 150.075 × _____ = 1,500.75

Name _____

Estimating Length

Estimate first, then measure.

1. How wide is a classroom door?

Estimate: _____ dm

Measure: _____ dm

2. How long is your pencil?

Estimate: _____ cm

Measure: _____ cm

3. How long is your little finger?

Estimate: _____ cm

Measure: _____ cm

4. How wide is your chair?

Estimate: _____ dm

Measure: _____ dm

5. How wide is your smile?

Estimate: _____ cm

Measure: _____ cm

6. How long is your ear?

Estimate: _____ cm

Measure: _____ cm

7. How wide is this paper?

Estimate: _____ dm

Measure: _____ dm

8. What is the height from the floor to the ceiling?

Estimate: _____ m

Measure: _____ m

9. How thick is your math book?

Estimate: _____ cm

Measure: _____ cm

10. How long is a jumbo paper clip?

Estimate: _____ cm

Measure: _____ cm

Name _____

Meters and Centimeters

Write each measurement two ways. First use only
centimeters. Then use only meters.

1. 4 m 52 cm _____   **2.** 1 m 9 cm _____   **3.** 6 m 72 cm _____

_____   _____   _____

4. 9 m 50 cm _____   **5.** 10 m 38 cm _____   **6.** 7 m 95 cm _____

_____   _____

Give the missing numbers.

7. 856 cm = _____ m   **8.** 6.5 m = _____ cm   **9.** 125 cm = _____ m

Change each measure to meters.

10. Refrigerator height _____

11. Refrigerator width _____

12. Refrigerator depth _____

Change each measure to centimeters.

13. Cupboard height _____

14. Cupboard width _____

15. Cupboard depth _____

Centimeters and Millimeters

Use both centimeter and millimeter units to write the length shown.

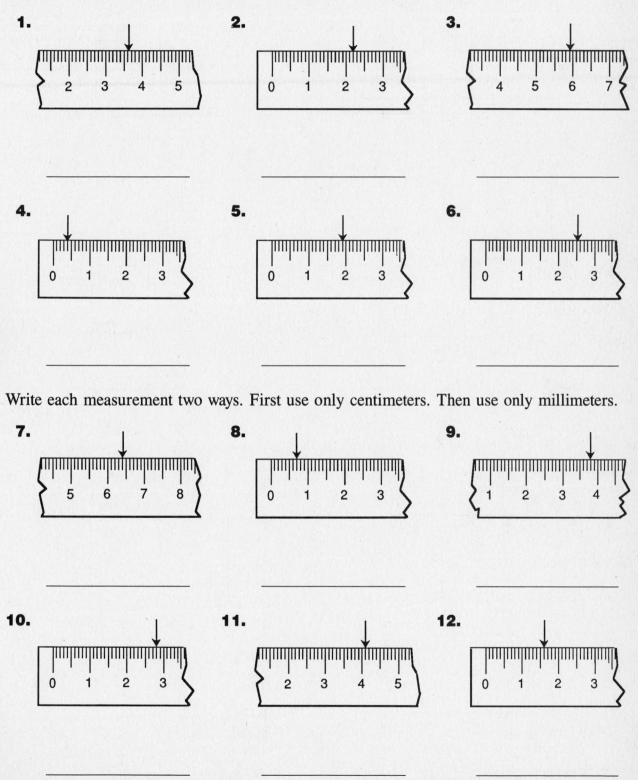

1.

_____

2.

_____

3.

_____

4.

_____

5.

_____

6.

_____

Write each measurement two ways. First use only centimeters. Then use only millimeters.

7.

_____

8.

_____

9.

_____

10.

_____

11.

_____

12.

_____

Area of a Rectangle

Find the area for each rectangle.

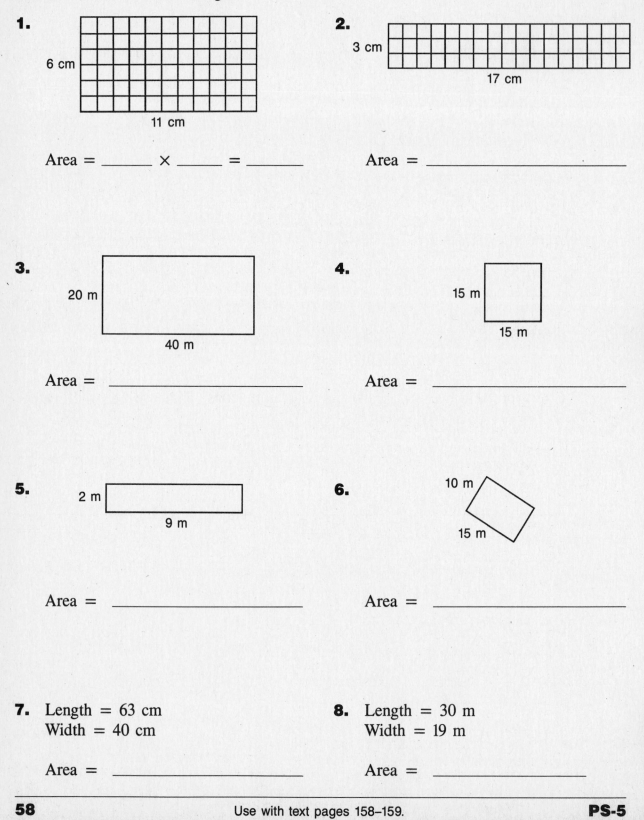

1.

6 cm

11 cm

Area = _____ × _____ = _____

2.

3 cm

17 cm

Area = _____

3.

20 m

40 m

Area = _____

4.

15 m

15 m

Area = _____

5.

2 m

9 m

Area = _____

6.

10 m

15 m

Area = _____

7. Length = 63 cm
Width = 40 cm

Area = _____

8. Length = 30 m
Width = 19 m

Area = _____

Kilometers

Write the correct unit (m or km).

1. A very tall Coast Redwood tree is 110 _____ tall.

2. Sears Tower in Chicago is 443 _____ tall.

3. The distance between London and New Delhi is 6,727 _____ .

4. The ship *Queen Elizabeth 2* is 294 _____ long.

5. The Allegheny River is 523 _____ long.

6. The statue of William Penn at City Hall Tower in Philadelphia is

11 _____ tall.

7. The distance between New York and Rome is 6,907 _____ .

8. At its lowest point the Dead Sea is 397 _____ below sea level.

Give each distance in kilometers using decimals.

9. The average depth of the Pacific Ocean is 4,188 m. _____

10. Mt. Kilimanjaro is 5,895 m high.   _____

11. The Golden Gate Bridge is 1,280 m long.   _____

12. The Gateway to the West Arch in St. Louis is
192 m long.   _____

Name _____

Capacity and Volume

Ring the best estimate for the capacity of each container.

1.   **2.**   **3.**

5 mL	1.25 L	100 mL
500 mL	12.5 L	10 L
5,000 mL	125 L	100 L

Complete each equation.

4. 3,000 mL = ____ L   **5.** 7,000 mL = ____ L   **6.** 9,000 mL = ____ L

7. 3 L = _____ mL   **8.** 7 L = _____ mL   **9.** 9 L = _____ mL

10. 3 mL = _____ L   **11.** 7 mL = _____ L   **12.** 9 mL = _____ L

13. 720 mL = _____ L   **14.** 64 mL = _____ L   **15.** 0.326 L = ____ mL

Solve.

16. Maxine's water bottle holds 1.5 L. How many milliliters is this?

17. If Maxine filled her water bottle 4 times on a hike, how many milliliters of water did she use?

Name _____

Kilograms and Grams

Give the missing numbers.

1. math book

2. dog food

3. salt

800 g = _____ kg

5.43 kg = _____ g

_____ kg = 737 g

4. glass of water

5. baseball

6. flour

0.25 kg = _____ g

150 g = _____ kg

2,300 g = _____ kg

7. bowling ball

8. pitcher of milk

9. scissors

7 kg = _____ g

_____ g = 1 kg

_____ kg = 100 g

Make an Organized List

Solve. Use any problem-solving strategy.

```
YAHOO YOGURT

Today's Flavors          Toppings—$0.50 each
Viva Vanilla             Granola
Sassy Strawberry         Pecans
Bodacious Banana         Raspberries
                         Strawberries

small—$1.00      medium—$1.75      large—$2.50
```

1. Louis wanted a medium vanilla with two different toppings. How many possible choices did he have?   _____

2. Maria knew she did not want any toppings, but she could not decide which flavor to choose or what size to get. How many choices did she have?   _____

3. Arthur could not go to Yahoo Yogurt. He asked Maria to bring him a large of any flavor with two different toppings. How many choices did Maria have?   _____

4. Brent ordered a small strawberry with two toppings for himself and a medium vanilla with no toppings for his little sister. How much change did he get from a $10 bill?   _____

5. Lisa works at Yahoo Yogurt three afternoons a week from 4 to 6 in the afternoon. She is paid $3.50 an hour. How much does she earn in four weeks?   _____

6. Martha delivered coupons. She gave one packet of coupons to each of 26 stores. She delivered a total of 1,950 coupons. How many coupons were in each packet?   _____

Time

Give the time in days and hours.

1. 50 h _____

2. 72 h _____

3. 30 h _____

4. 60 h _____

5. 48 h _____

6. 90 h _____

Give the time in hours and minutes.

7. 72 min _____

8. 80 min _____

9. 360 min _____

10. 105 min _____

11. 270 min _____

12. 180 min _____

Give the time in minutes and seconds.

13. 83 s _____

14. 130 s _____

15. 175 s _____

16. 300 s _____

17. 215 s _____

18. 68 s _____

Give the time in seconds only.

19. 2 min 5 s _____

20. 1 min 30 s _____

21. 4 min 15 s _____

22. 3 min 2 s _____

23. 2 min 59 s _____

24. 3 min 20 s _____

Write < or > to indicate which time is faster for
each race.

25. 8-kilometer race

1,498 s ◯ 24 min

26. 10-kilometer race

28 min ◯ 1,702 s

27. marathon

2 h 17 min ◯ 135 min

Name _____

Problem Solving: Using Data from a Thermometer

Write the temperature (°C) shown on each thermometer.

1.

90
85
80
75

Hot tea

_____

2.

15
10
5
0

Iced tea

_____

3.

15
10
5
0

Winter day

_____

4.

40
35
30
25

Body temperature

_____

5.

10
5
0
-5

Block of ice

_____

6.

125
120
115
110

Cooking stew

_____

7.

30
25
20
15

Swimming pool

_____

8.

40
35
30
25

Hot bath

_____

9.

200
195
190
185

Oven temperature

_____

Special Quotients

Divide.

1. $180 \div 6 \ = \ $_____ **2.** $160 \div 2 \ = \ $_____ **3.** $120 \div 4 \ = \ $_____

4. $140 \div 7 \ = \ $_____ **5.** $240 \div 4 \ = \ $_____ **6.** $140 \div 2 \ = \ $_____

7. $120 \div 2 \ = \ $_____ **8.** $180 \div 3 \ = \ $_____ **9.** $160 \div 8 \ = \ $_____

10. $3{,}600 \div 9 \ = \ $_____ **11.** $2{,}700 \div 3 \ = \ $_____ **12.** $2{,}100 \div 7 \ = \ $_____

13. $3{,}200 \div 8 \ = \ $_____ **14.** $2{,}800 \div 4 \ = \ $_____ **15.** $1{,}200 \div 6 \ = \ $_____

16. $2{,}400 \div 8 \ = \ $_____ **17.** $1{,}200 \div 3 \ = \ $_____ **18.** $1{,}500 \div 3 \ = \ $_____

19. $35{,}000 \div 5 = \ $_____ **20.** $36{,}000 \div 6 = \ $_____ **21.** $18{,}000 \div 9 = \ $_____

22. $15{,}000 \div 5 = \ $_____ **23.** $28{,}000 \div 7 = \ $_____ **24.** $24{,}000 \div 3 = \ $_____

25. $240 \div 6 \ = \ $_____ **26.** $630 \div 9 \ = \ $_____ **27.** $160 \div 4 \ = \ $_____

28. $4{,}800 \div 6 \ = \ $_____ **29.** $4{,}200 \div 7 \ = \ $_____ **30.** $6{,}400 \div 8 \ = \ $_____

31. $35{,}000 \div 7 = \ $_____ **32.** $56{,}000 \div 8 = \ $_____ **33.** $72{,}000 \div 9 = \ $_____

34. Find the quotient of 2,500 and 5. _____

35. What is 36,000 divided by 9? _____

36. What is 5,400 divided by 6? _____

37. Find the quotient of 48,000 and 8. _____

38. Find the quotient of 2,100 and 3. _____

39. What is 8,100 divided by 9? _____

Estimating Quotients: Rounding and Compatible Numbers

Which would be a better choice for estimating the
quotient? Write **A** or **B**.

1. $589 \div 8$ _____   **A** $560 \div 8$ **B** $640 \div 8$

2. $692 \div 9$ _____   **A** $720 \div 9$ **B** $630 \div 9$

3. $256 \div 4$ _____   **A** $240 \div 4$ **B** $280 \div 4$

4. $362 \div 7$ _____   **A** $420 \div 7$ **B** $350 \div 7$

5. $444 \div 5$ _____   **A** $400 \div 5$ **B** $450 \div 5$

6. $1{,}735 \div 6$ _____   **A** $1{,}800 \div 6$ **B** $1{,}200 \div 6$

7. $896 \div 9$ _____   **A** $810 \div 9$ **B** $900 \div 9$

8. $1{,}678 \div 7$ _____   **A** $1{,}400 \div 7$ **B** $2{,}100 \div 7$

9. $2{,}602 \div 5$ _____   **A** $3{,}000 \div 5$ **B** $2{,}500 \div 5$

10. $4{,}981 \div 8$ _____   **A** $4{,}800 \div 8$ **B** $5{,}600 \div 8$

Estimate each quotient by substituting compatible
numbers.

11. $752 \div 9$ _____   **12.** $463 \div 9$ _____

13. $375 \div 6$ _____   **14.** $213 \div 7$ _____

15. $5{,}814 \div 8$ _____   **16.** $2{,}987 \div 5$ _____

17. $1{,}233 \div 3$ _____   **18.** $3{,}952 \div 4$ _____

19. $4{,}398 \div 6$ _____   **20.** $6{,}825 \div 9$ _____

Dividing Whole Numbers: Making the Connection

Find each quotient using place value blocks. Record
your work using symbols.

1. $60 \div 4 =$ _____

2. $32 \div 2 =$ _____

3. $30 \div 2 =$ _____

4. $42 \div 2 =$ _____

5. $18 \div 3 =$ _____

6. $36 \div 3 =$ _____

7. $15 \div 3 =$ _____

8. $64 \div 4 =$ _____

9. $45 \div 3 =$ _____

Each picture shows the result *after* dividing. Write
the original division problem.

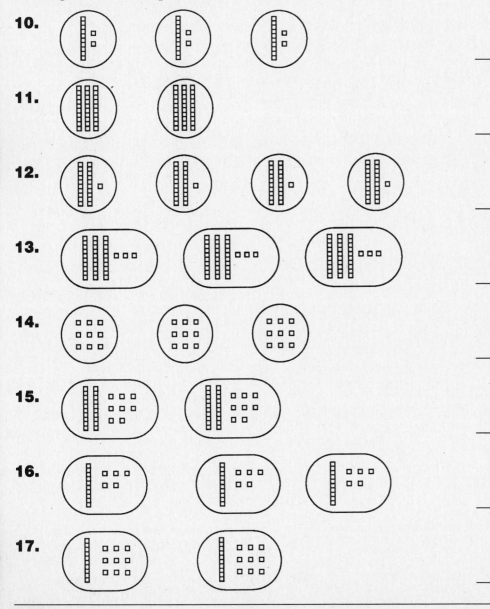

10. _____

11. _____

12. _____

13. _____

14. _____

15. _____

16. _____

17. _____

Dividing 2- and 3-Digit Quotients

Divide.

1. $5\overline{)62}$ **2.** $4\overline{)45}$ **3.** $6\overline{)87}$ **4.** $8\overline{)92}$

5. $875 \div 6$ **6.** $555 \div 4$ **7.** $623 \div 5$

Use mental math to find each quotient.

8. $2\overline{)480}$ **9.** $6\overline{)3,600}$ **10.** $3\overline{)180}$ **11.** $7\overline{)5,600}$

Dividing: Deciding Where to Start

Where do you start dividing? Choose the hundreds place or the tens place.

1. $6\overline{)740}$ _____

2. $8\overline{)578}$ _____

3. $9\overline{)626}$ _____

4. $7\overline{)597}$ _____

5. $6\overline{)703}$ _____

6. $6\overline{)524}$ _____

Divide.

7. $9\overline{)588}$

8. $5\overline{)371}$

9. $7\overline{)478}$

10. $8\overline{)619}$

11. $6\overline{)500}$

12. $7\overline{)659}$

13. $8\overline{)512}$

14. $9\overline{)686}$

Use mental math to find each quotient.

15. $9\overline{)729}$

16. $7\overline{)284}$

17. $6\overline{)612}$

18. $4\overline{)816}$

Dividing: Special Cases

Divide.

1. $7\overline{)755}$ **2.** $3\overline{)931}$ **3.** $5\overline{)404}$ **4.** $4\overline{)683}$

5. $4\overline{)2,808}$ **6.** $6\overline{)2,640}$ **7.** $3\overline{)1,509}$ **8.** $9\overline{)7,209}$

Find each quotient using mental math.

9. $560 \div 8$ _____   **10.** $2,100 \div 7$ _____   **11.** $63,000 \div 9$ _____

Name _____

Finding Averages

Find the average of these distances.

1. 46, 17, 33   **2.** 51, 24, 18   **3.** 35, 12, 25

4. 85, 74, 28, 49   **5.** 91, 13, 55, 77   **6.** 45, 61, 62, 36

7. 71, 36, 48, 40, 15   **8.** 21, 19, 11, 17, 12   **9.** 43, 26, 89, 21, 76

Name _____

Interpreting Remainders

Solve. Use any problem solving strategy.

1. There were 90 campers at tennis camp. There were 17 instructors. Every instructor taught a group. Most groups had 5 campers. How many groups had 6 campers?

2. Lorna was preparing the day's snack packs. Each was to contain 8 sandwiches. The lunch service delivered 180 sandwiches. How many full packs could Lorna prepare?

3. Mary wanted to buy tennis balls. She saved $24. A can of balls cost $5 on sale. How many cans could she buy?

4. A counselor worked 8 hours on Monday, 9 hours on Wednesday, 6 hours on Thursday, and 12 hours on Friday. She had Tuesday off. How many hours of work per day did she average over the 5-day week?

5. All 90 campers and 17 instructors went to a game on Sunday afternoon. They traveled by van. Each van holds 9 people. How many vans were needed?

6. Wristbands come in a pack of six. How many packs were needed to provide each of the 107 people at camp with one wrist band?

7. The campers sleep four in a cabin. How many cabins were needed for the 90 campers?

8. Hugh had $5 to spend on treats for the four boys in his cabin. How much could he spend per person?

9. Scott went to several stores looking for tennis shorts. He found them priced for $35, $21, $16, and $10. What was the average price?

10. The campers bought discount tickets for the County Fair. The tickets were 20 for $15. How much did they spend for tickets?

Work Backward

Work backward to help you solve each problem.

1. William counted the legs on a centipede. He told Max, "If you multiply the number of legs by 2 and divide by 7, you get 8." How many legs did the centipede have?

_____

2. Boris had seen an amazing starfish at the science museum. He said, "If you add 14 to the number of arms on this starfish and then divide by 16, you get 4." How many arms did the starfish have?

_____

3. Max counted the legs on a caterpillar and said, "If you divide the number of caterpillar legs by 4 and multiply by 25, you get 100." How many legs did the caterpillar have?

_____

4. Rachel said she had a mystery pet at home. When her friends asked her how many legs her pet had, she said, "If you multiply the number by 4 and then divide by 8, you get 2." How many legs does Rachel's pet have?

_____

5. Julie noticed that butterflies and caterpillars have different numbers of legs. If you take the number of butterfly legs, multiply by 8, and then divide by 12, you will get 4." How many legs do butterflies have?

_____

6. Wes said, "I have a pet just like yours and she had kittens. My sister is planning to sell each kitten for $5. Then we'll make $30." How many kittens did Wes's cat have?

_____

7. Meghan said, "If you subtract 5 from the number of legs on a shrimp and then add 18, you get 23." How many legs does a shrimp have?

_____

8. Keesha said, "My sister has had her cat since she was a little girl. If you multiply the cat's age by 3 and then divide by 9, you get 5." How old is the cat?

_____

Dividing Decimals: Making the Connection

The money in the pictures has been divided into equal groups. Write the division problem and the answer for each group.

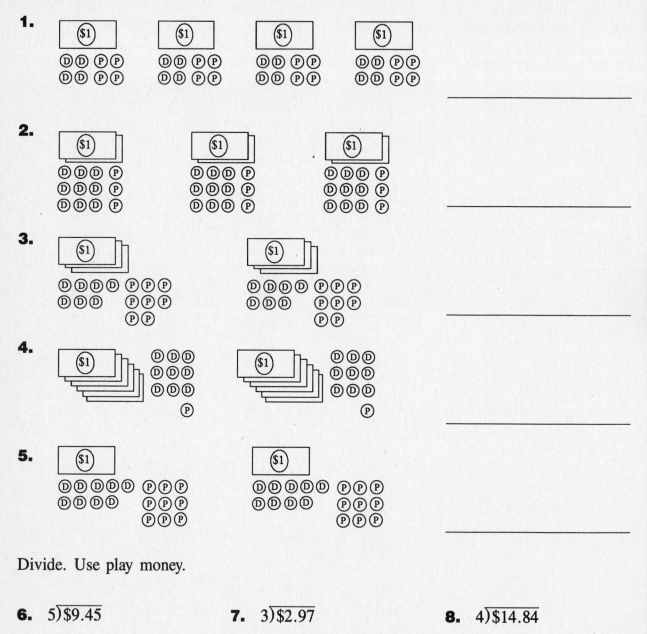

1.

2.

3.

4.

5.

Divide. Use play money.

6. 5)$9.45

7. 3)$2.97

8. 4)$14.84

Use with text pages 198–199.

Name _____

Dividing Decimals

Divide.

1. $5\overline{)7.25}$ **2.** $6\overline{)1.872}$ **3.** $3\overline{)15.48}$ **4.** $8\overline{)51.2}$

5. $9\overline{)287.1}$ **6.** $4\overline{)12.44}$ **7.** $2\overline{)1.108}$ **8.** $5\overline{)123.0}$

Use mental math to find each quotient.

9. $45.05 \div 5$ _____ **10.** $3.6 \div 6$ _____ **11.** $14.63 \div 7$ _____

Use with text pages 200–201.

Name _____

Determining Reasonable Answers

Do not solve the problems. Decide whether the answer
shown on the calculator is reasonable. Write **yes**
or **no** for each problem and explain your answer.

1. The coach brought 20 baseballs to
practice. Jay carried the ball bag. If
one baseball weighs 5.5 oz, how
much did the bag weigh?

_____

_____

$$1000$$

2. Sam's dad told him his bowling ball
weighed 256 oz. There are 16 oz in
a pound. How many pounds does the
bowling ball weigh?

_____

_____

$$16$$

3. The gym teacher gave Nadia a box
of 30 softballs to distribute to the
classrooms. If one softball weighs
6.25 oz, how much did the box
weigh?

_____

4. Ashley collects lost golf balls. One
day she found 28 balls. If one golf
ball weighs 1.62 oz, how much did
all 28 weigh?

_____

$$45.36$$

5. Deanna collected all the tennis balls
after her lesson. There were 75
tennis balls. One ball weighs about
58.5 g. How much did the ball
basket weigh?

_____

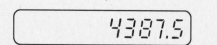

6. Adria's croquet set has 8 balls. If one
ball weighs 16.25 oz, how many
ounces does the set of 8 weigh?

_____

_____

Special Quotients

Divide and check.

1. $6 \div 2$ = _____

2. $60 \div 20$ = _____

3. $6,000 \div 20$ = ___

4. $12 \div 4$ = _____

5. $120 \div 40$ = _____

6. $1,200 \div 400$ = ___

7. $14 \div 7$ = _____

8. $140 \div 70$ = _____

9. $1,400 \div 700$ = ___

10. $72 \div 8$ = _____

11. $720 \div 80$ = _____

12. $7,200 \div 80$ = ___

13. $36 \div 9$ = _____

14. $360 \div 90$ = _____

15. $3,600 \div 900$ = ___

16. $56 \div 8$ = _____

17. $560 \div 80$ = _____

18. $5,600 \div 80$ = ___

19. $45 \div 9$ = _____

20. $450 \div 90$ = _____

21. $4,500 \div 90$ = ___

22. $80\overline{)640}$

23. $60\overline{)480}$

24. $50\overline{)300}$

25. $20\overline{)140}$

26. $90\overline{)180}$

27. $40\overline{)160}$

28. $50\overline{)250}$

29. $90\overline{)270}$

30. $50\overline{)450}$

31. $90\overline{)810}$

32. $80\overline{)400}$

33. $40\overline{)320}$

34. $30\overline{)2,400}$

35. $60\overline{)3,600}$

36. $40\overline{)2,800}$

37. $80\overline{)3,200}$

38. $70\overline{)2,100}$

39. $30\overline{)1,200}$

40. $40\overline{)3,600}$

41. $60\overline{)4,200}$

Estimating Quotient Digits

Which front-end digits would you use to
estimate the quotient digit?

1. $90\overline{)375}$

2. $40\overline{)387}$

3. $70\overline{)592}$

_____   _____   _____

4. $80\overline{)319}$

5. $60\overline{)95}$

6. $20\overline{)168}$

_____   _____   _____

7. $80\overline{)683}$

8. $30\overline{)689}$

9. $50\overline{)673}$

_____   _____   _____

10. If the first digit of the divisor is larger than the first
digit of the dividend, how many digits of the dividend
do you use in your estimate?   _____

Estimate the quotient.   **Example:** $50\overline{)367}$ with quotient 7 and 350
Multiply to check.

11. $20\overline{)132}$

12. $50\overline{)271}$

13. $90\overline{)223}$

_____   _____   _____

14. $70\overline{)182}$

15. $30\overline{)251}$

16. $60\overline{)457}$

_____   _____   _____

17. $50\overline{)484}$

18. $80\overline{)603}$

19. $40\overline{)178}$

_____   _____   _____

Dividing: 1-Digit Quotients

Divide.

1. $48\overline{)446}$ **2.** $74\overline{)453}$ **3.** $38\overline{)316}$ **4.** $29\overline{)269}$

5. $59\overline{)323}$ **6.** $87\overline{)788}$ **7.** $69\overline{)304}$ **8.** $97\overline{)591}$

9. $46\overline{)265}$ **10.** $58\overline{)561}$ **11.** $37\overline{)321}$ **12.** $42\overline{)241}$

13. $157 \div 18$ **14.** $275 \div 35$ **15.** $757 \div 82$

Name _____

Changing Estimates

Divide.

1. $48\overline{)312}$ **2.** $66\overline{)325}$ **3.** $72\overline{)419}$ **4.** $57\overline{)482}$

5. $73\overline{)505}$ **6.** $38\overline{)181}$ **7.** $75\overline{)333}$ **8.** $76\overline{)266}$

9. $83\overline{)367}$ **10.** $64\overline{)634}$ **11.** $87\overline{)511}$ **12.** $75\overline{)483}$

13. $400 \div 59$ **14.** $347 \div 45$ **15.** $518 \div 63$

Finding Larger Quotients

Divide.

1. $22\overline{)825}$ **2.** $38\overline{)763}$ **3.** $73\overline{)4,929}$

4. $43\overline{)6,721}$ **5.** $24\overline{)7,808}$ **6.** $51\overline{)8,392}$

7. $725 \div 27$ **8.** $3,257 \div 49$ **9.** $5,023 \div 44$

Choosing a Calculation Method

Choose an appropriate calculation method. Then solve.

1. John paid $117 for 6 shirts. About how much did each shirt cost?

_____

2. During a 9-day period, the clothing store paid clerks for 267 hours of work. About how many hours of work did the store pay for each day?

_____

3. A clothing store bought 9 sweaters for $186. About how much did each sweater cost?

_____

4. The store manager paid $441 for a rack of $9 ties. How many ties were on the rack?

_____

5. Bill put 8 boxes of socks in each bin. How many bins did he fill with 568 boxes?

_____

6. Jill hung $336 worth of skirts on 8 hangers. Each skirt cost the same. How much did each skirt cost?

_____

7. One week (6 days), 534 customers bought items from the clothing store. About how many customers bought items each day?

_____

8. The clothing store is open 300 days a year. If it is open 7 days a week, how many weeks is it open?

_____

9. The store paid Ted $187.50 for 6 days' work. How much did he make per day?

_____

10. Verna bought a box of 4 barrettes for $2.76. What was the cost for each barrette?

_____

11. Mrs. Howell bought jackets for her family. She paid $283 for 4 jackets. About how much did each jacket cost?

_____

12. Carla ordered 7 items for a special store display. The total cost was $577.50. Each item cost the same. How much did each item cost?

_____

Name _____

Dividing: Special Cases

Divide.

1. $27\overline{)8,280}$

2. $41\overline{)16,615}$

3. $56\overline{)37,544}$

4. $38\overline{)19,120}$

5. $62\overline{)4,989}$

6. $93\overline{)3,798}$

7. $24,700 \div 35$

8. $4,055 \div 67$

9. $9,560 \div 19$

Name _____

Looking for a Pattern

Look for a pattern to help you solve each problem.
Use the chart to record the pattern.

1. Mattie was very tired after swimming five laps.
She decided to increase her stamina by swimming
one more lap each day. She decided to begin the
following Monday and swim five days a week.
If she followed her plan, how many laps would
she swim at the end of eight weeks?

_____

Week	0	1	2	3	4	5	6	7	8
Laps	5	10							

2. At the awards ceremony every member of
Brent's team shook hands with every other
member. There were eleven members of the
team. How many handshakes were there?

_____

Members	1	2	3	4	5	6	7	8	9	10	11
Handshakes											

3. Lauren had to record the temperature every
seven hours for her science experiment. She
started recording at 1:00 p.m. What time was
her fourth reading?

_____

Recording	1	2	3	4
Time				

Dividing Decimals by 10, 100, and 1,000

Divide each number by 10, by 100, and then by 1,000.

		Divide by 10	Divide by 100	Divide by 1,000
1.	1,000	_____	_____	_____
2.	100	_____	_____	_____
3.	10	_____	_____	_____
4.	7,532	_____	_____	_____
5.	753.2	_____	_____	_____
6.	75.32	_____	_____	_____
7.	450	_____	_____	_____
8.	45	_____	_____	_____
9.	4.5	_____	_____	_____
10.	5,366.4	_____	_____	_____
11.	7,028.9	_____	_____	_____
12.	355.1	_____	_____	_____
13.	906.2	_____	_____	_____
14.	3,852.7	_____	_____	_____
15.	65.8	_____	_____	_____
16.	49.3	_____	_____	_____

Estimating the Answer

Estimate the answer to these problems.

1. Ms. Eckert travels 324 km to and from work each week. How far does she travel in 8 weeks?

_____

2. Mr. Esposito drove at an average speed of 82 km per hour for 9 hours. About how far did he drive?

_____

3. Vito can swim an average of 52 m per minute. He can run an average of 212 m per minute. About how many more meters can he run than swim in 6 minutes.

_____

4. Sandy drove an average of 77 km per hour for 2 hours. Then she rode a train traveling at an average speed of 104 km per hour for 3 hours About how far did she travel?

_____

5. Tracy walked an average of 78 m per minute for 27 minutes. About how far did she walk?

_____

6. A train traveled an average speed of 98 km per hour for 8 hours. About how far did it travel?

_____

7. Rodrigo jogged an average of 176 m per minute for 18 minutes. About how far did he jog?

_____

8. Linda swam an average of 48 m per minute for 22 minutes. About how far did she swim?

_____

9. Darlene walked an average of 71 m per minute for 9 minutes. Then she ran an average of 257 m per minute for 4 minutes. About how far did Darlene go?

_____

10. If a car traveling an average of 88 km per hour and a ship traveling an average of 52 km per hour each traveled for 4 hours, about how much farther would the car go?

_____

Name _____

Reviewing the Meaning of Fractions

Write the fraction for the shaded part.

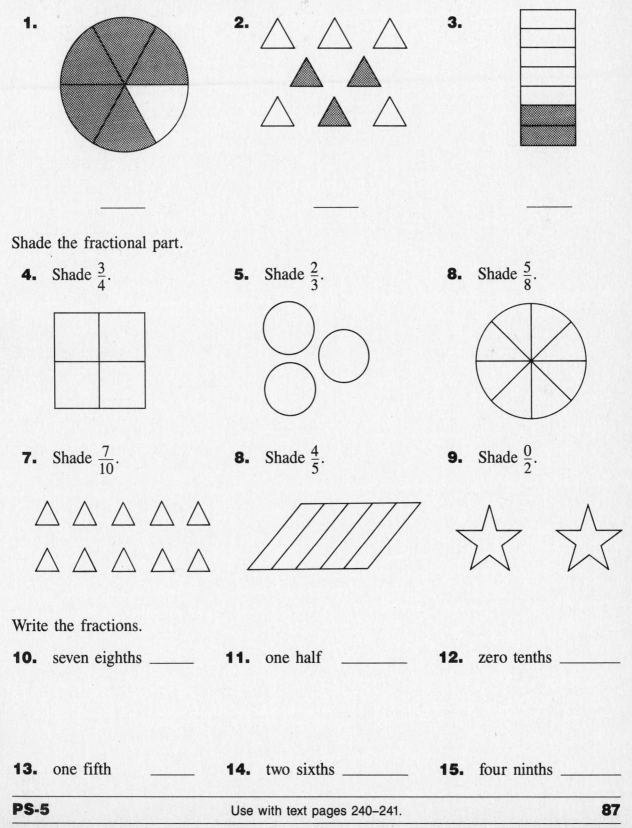

1.

_____

2.

_____

3.

_____

Shade the fractional part.

4. Shade $\frac{3}{4}$.

5. Shade $\frac{2}{3}$.

8. Shade $\frac{5}{8}$.

7. Shade $\frac{7}{10}$.

8. Shade $\frac{4}{5}$.

9. Shade $\frac{0}{2}$.

Write the fractions.

10. seven eighths _____

11. one half _____

12. zero tenths _____

13. one fifth _____

14. two sixths _____

15. four ninths _____

Name _____

Equivalent Fractions

Write two fractions that name the shaded part of each region or set.

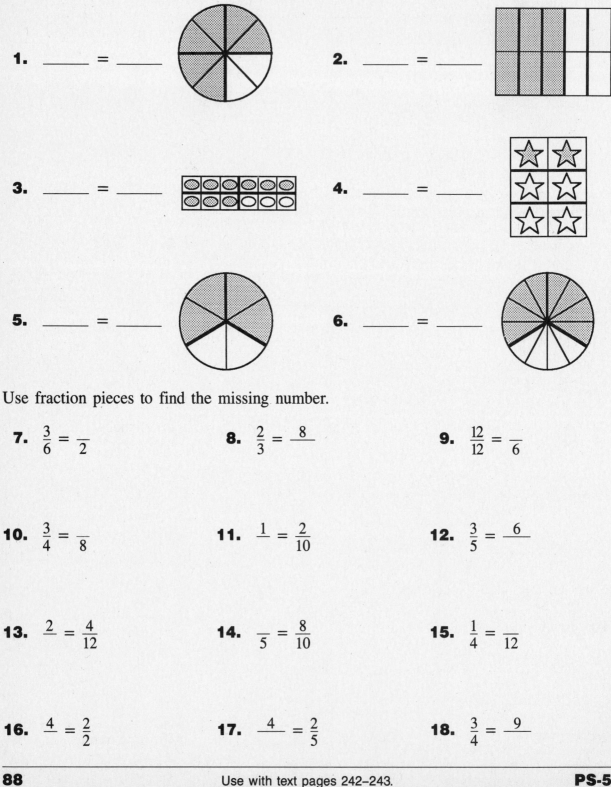

1. _____ = _____

2. _____ = _____

3. _____ = _____

4. _____ = _____

5. _____ = _____

6. _____ = _____

Use fraction pieces to find the missing number.

7. $\frac{3}{6} = \frac{}{2}$

8. $\frac{2}{3} = \frac{8}{}$

9. $\frac{12}{12} = \frac{}{6}$

10. $\frac{3}{4} = \frac{}{8}$

11. $\frac{1}{} = \frac{2}{10}$

12. $\frac{3}{5} = \frac{6}{}$

13. $\frac{2}{} = \frac{4}{12}$

14. $\frac{}{5} = \frac{8}{10}$

15. $\frac{1}{4} = \frac{}{12}$

16. $\frac{4}{} = \frac{2}{2}$

17. $\frac{4}{} = \frac{2}{5}$

18. $\frac{3}{4} = \frac{9}{}$

Name _____

Finding Equivalent Fractions

Find equivalent fractions by multiplying the
numerator and denominator by 3.

1. $\dfrac{2}{3} =$ _____   **2.** $\dfrac{3}{4} =$ _____   **3.** $\dfrac{1}{6} =$ _____   **4.** $\dfrac{2}{5} =$ _____

Find equivalent fractions by multiplying the
numerator and denominator by 5.

5. $\dfrac{1}{6} =$ _____   **6.** $\dfrac{2}{5} =$ _____   **7.** $\dfrac{5}{6} =$ _____   **8.** $\dfrac{3}{7} =$ _____

Tell by what number the numerator and denominator were
multiplied to get the equivalent fraction.

9. $\dfrac{2}{3} = \dfrac{8}{12}$ _____   **10.** $\dfrac{3}{5} = \dfrac{12}{20}$ _____   **11.** $\dfrac{3}{4} = \dfrac{18}{24}$ _____

12. $\dfrac{5}{7} = \dfrac{10}{14}$ _____   **13.** $\dfrac{1}{6} = \dfrac{3}{18}$ _____   **14.** $\dfrac{4}{5} = \dfrac{20}{25}$ _____

Write an equivalent fraction.

15. $\dfrac{1}{2} = \dfrac{}{10}$ **16.** $\dfrac{1}{3} = \dfrac{}{9}$ **17.** $\dfrac{5}{8} = \dfrac{}{24}$ **18.** $\dfrac{3}{10} = \dfrac{}{30}$

19. $\dfrac{1}{10} = \dfrac{}{70}$ **20.** $\dfrac{1}{5} = \dfrac{}{40}$ **21.** $\dfrac{5}{6} = \dfrac{}{24}$ **22.** $\dfrac{2}{9} = \dfrac{}{36}$

Write the next three equivalent fractions in the pattern.

23. $\dfrac{2}{3}, \dfrac{4}{6},$ _____, _____, _____   **24.** $\dfrac{3}{7}, \dfrac{6}{14},$ _____, _____, _____

25. $\dfrac{1}{2}, \dfrac{2}{4},$ _____, _____, _____   **26.** $\dfrac{7}{8}, \dfrac{14}{16},$ _____, _____, _____

Greatest Common Factor

Find the greatest common factor.

1. List the factors of 18. _____

2. List the factors of 24. _____

3. List the common factors of 18 and 24. _____

4. Give the greatest common factor of 18 and 24. _____

5. List the factors of 12. _____

6. List the factors of 20. _____

7. List the common factors of 12 and 20. _____

8. Give the greatest common factor of 12 and 20. _____

List the factors of each number. Ring the greatest
common factor or each pair.

9. 8 _____

28 _____

10. 20 _____

16 _____

11. 40 _____

24 _____

12. 36 _____

27 _____

13. 21 _____

15 _____

14. 11 _____

26 _____

15. 48 _____

16 _____

16. 18 _____

21 _____

Lowest-Terms Fractions

Tell whether the fraction is in lowest terms. Write **yes** or **no.**

1. $\frac{3}{15}$ _____

2. $\frac{2}{7}$ _____

3. $\frac{9}{16}$ _____

4. $\frac{8}{32}$ _____

5. $\frac{25}{35}$ _____

6. $\frac{10}{13}$ _____

7. $\frac{4}{20}$ _____

8. $\frac{16}{21}$ _____

9. $\frac{6}{27}$ _____

Reduce to lowest terms when not already in lowest terms.

10. $\frac{12}{36}$ _____

11. $\frac{18}{63}$ _____

12. $\frac{4}{15}$ _____

13. $\frac{16}{72}$ _____

14. $\frac{6}{35}$ _____

15. $\frac{9}{30}$ _____

16. $\frac{4}{16}$ _____

17. $\frac{7}{28}$ _____

18. $\frac{40}{70}$ _____

19. $\frac{3}{18}$ _____

20. $\frac{8}{21}$ _____

21. $\frac{34}{50}$ _____

22. $\frac{9}{12}$ _____

23. $\frac{21}{35}$ _____

24. $\frac{16}{40}$ _____

25. $\frac{12}{25}$ _____

26. $\frac{9}{24}$ _____

27. $\frac{13}{20}$ _____

28. $\frac{6}{16}$ _____

29. $\frac{16}{30}$ _____

30. $\frac{50}{75}$ _____

31. $\frac{18}{27}$ _____

32. $\frac{40}{100}$ _____

33. $\frac{24}{42}$ _____

Exploring Algebra: More About Variables

Complete each table. Then describe the pattern you used.

1.

x	0	1	2	3	4	5	6
y	0	4	8				

$y =$ _____

2.

s	0	1	2	3	4	5	6
t	0	$\frac{1}{2}$	1				

$t =$ _____

3.

c	0	1	2	3	4	5	6
d	10	11	12				

$d =$ _____

4.

m	0	1	2	3	4	5	6
n	0	1	4				

$n =$ _____

5.

x	0	1	2	3	4	5	6
y	0	10	20				

$y =$ _____

6.

s	0	1	2	3	4	5	6
t	3	6	9				

$t =$ _____

7.

c	0	1	2	3	4	5	6
d	5	7	9				

$d =$ _____

8.

m	0	1	2	3	4	5	6
n	0	5	10				

$n =$ _____

Use Logical Reasoning

Use logical reasoning to solve these problems. The charts can help you organize your thinking.

1. Carlos (C), Valerie (V), Leigh (L), and Ben (B) were each born in a different state. One was born in Texas (TX), another in California (CA), another in Ohio (OH), and another in Arizona (AZ). Valerie and Leigh were not born in Arizona. Carlos was born in California. Ben was not born in Texas, and Leigh was not born in Ohio. Where was each person born?

	C	V	L	B
TX				
CA				
OH				
AZ				

_____

_____

2. Alexis's family has four dogs. One is a boxer (B), one is a German shepherd (GS), one is a golden retriever (GR), and the fourth is a cocker spaniel (CS). Their names are Tucker, Maybelle, Winston, and Lulu. The German shepherd's name is Lulu. The golden retriever's name is not Maybelle. The cocker spaniel's name is Tucker. What is the boxer's name?

	B	GS	GR	CS
Tucker				
Maybelle				
Winston				
Lulu				

_____

3. The Gregorio twins, Jennifer and Geoffrey, compete in soccer (SO), and tennis matches (T), swimming meets (SW), and basketball games (B). Each twin takes part in two sports that are different from the other twin's. Jennifer does not play tennis. Geoffrey does not play basketball. The twin who plays soccer plays basketball. In what sports does each twin compete?

	SO	T	SW	B
Jennifer				
Geoffrey				

_____

_____

_____

Name _____

Comparing and Ordering Fractions

Use fraction bars to compare the fractions. Then write < or > for each ◯.

1. (fraction bar for $\frac{1}{3}$) ➔

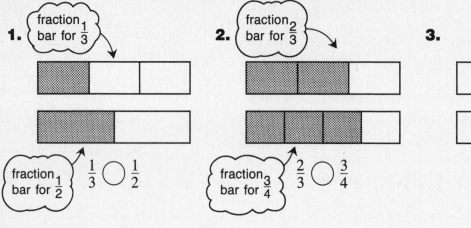

(fraction bar for $\frac{1}{2}$) ➔ $\frac{1}{3}$ ◯ $\frac{1}{2}$

2. (fraction bar for $\frac{2}{3}$) ➔

(fraction bar for $\frac{3}{4}$) ➔ $\frac{2}{3}$ ◯ $\frac{3}{4}$

3.

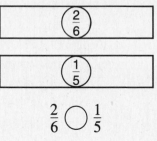

$\boxed{\frac{2}{6}}$

$\boxed{\frac{1}{5}}$

$\frac{2}{6}$ ◯ $\frac{1}{5}$

4.

$\boxed{\frac{3}{8}}$

$\boxed{\frac{2}{3}}$

$\frac{3}{8}$ ◯ $\frac{2}{3}$

5.

$\boxed{\frac{5}{8}}$

$\boxed{\frac{3}{4}}$

$\frac{5}{8}$ ◯ $\frac{3}{4}$

6.

$\boxed{\frac{7}{12}}$

$\boxed{\frac{5}{6}}$

$\frac{7}{12}$ ◯ $\frac{5}{6}$

Write <, >, or = for each ◯.

7. $\frac{2}{5}$ ◯ $\frac{3}{4}$ **8.** $\frac{5}{7}$ ◯ $\frac{2}{3}$ **9.** $\frac{7}{8}$ ◯ $\frac{9}{10}$ **10.** $\frac{3}{4}$ ◯ $\frac{7}{8}$

11. $\frac{4}{9}$ ◯ $\frac{17}{36}$ **12.** $\frac{5}{6}$ ◯ $\frac{8}{9}$ **13.** $\frac{3}{5}$ ◯ $\frac{6}{10}$ **14.** $\frac{13}{18}$ ◯ $\frac{5}{6}$

Write the fractions in order from greatest to least.

15. $\frac{3}{8}, \frac{1}{2}, \frac{1}{4}$ **16.** $\frac{3}{4}, \frac{5}{8}, \frac{1}{3}$ **17.** $\frac{2}{6}, \frac{7}{12}, \frac{3}{10}$

_____   _____   _____

Improper Fractions and Mixed Numbers: Using Manipulatives

Write the improper fraction and mixed number for the colored part of each picture.

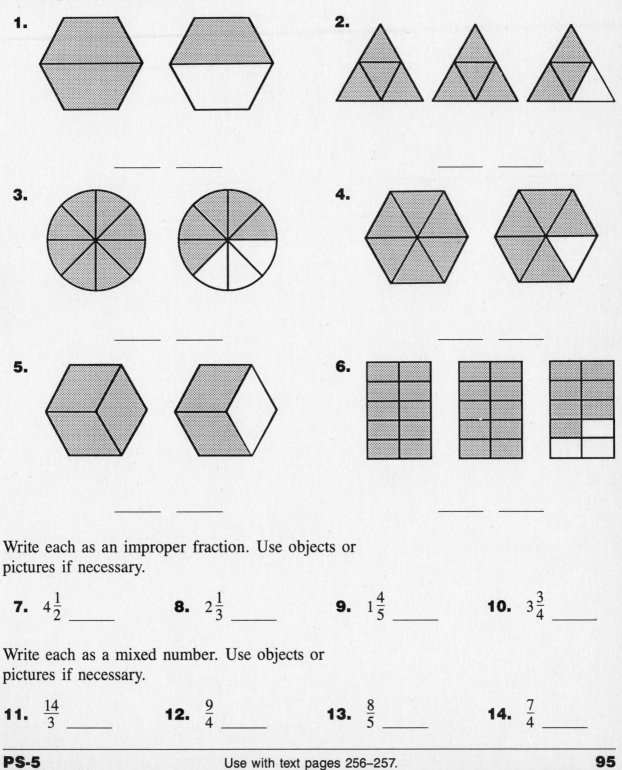

1.

_____ _____

2.

_____ _____

3.

_____ _____

4.

_____ _____

5.

_____ _____

6.

_____ _____

Write each as an improper fraction. Use objects or pictures if necessary.

7. $4\frac{1}{2}$ _____   **8.** $2\frac{1}{3}$ _____   **9.** $1\frac{4}{5}$ _____   **10.** $3\frac{3}{4}$ _____

Write each as a mixed number. Use objects or pictures if necessary.

11. $\frac{14}{3}$ _____   **12.** $\frac{9}{4}$ _____   **13.** $\frac{8}{5}$ _____   **14.** $\frac{7}{4}$ _____

More Improper Fractions and Mixed Numbers

Write each improper fraction as a whole number or as a mixed number.
Reduce the fraction to lowest terms.

1. $\dfrac{27}{3} =$ _____

2. $\dfrac{7}{5} =$ _____

3. $\dfrac{14}{10} =$ _____

4. $\dfrac{17}{16} =$ _____

5. $\dfrac{36}{6} =$ _____

6. $\dfrac{10}{3} =$ _____

7. $\dfrac{9}{6} =$ _____

8. $\dfrac{38}{6} =$ _____

9. $\dfrac{17}{8} =$ _____

10. $\dfrac{5}{2} =$ _____

11. $\dfrac{14}{4} =$ _____

12. $\dfrac{48}{12} =$ _____

13. $\dfrac{15}{5} =$ _____

14. $\dfrac{45}{10} =$ _____

15. $\dfrac{50}{8} =$ _____

Write each mixed number as an improper fraction.

16. $1\dfrac{1}{2}$ _____

17. $2\dfrac{1}{3}$ _____

18. $3\dfrac{1}{4}$ _____

19. $1\dfrac{2}{3}$ _____

20. $1\dfrac{3}{4}$ _____

21. $4\dfrac{1}{2}$ _____

22. $2\dfrac{1}{10}$ _____

23. $6\dfrac{1}{8}$ _____

24. $5\dfrac{1}{3}$ _____

25. $2\dfrac{3}{4}$ _____

26. $3\dfrac{3}{5}$ _____

27. $7\dfrac{3}{4}$ _____

28. $5\dfrac{7}{8}$ _____

29. $10\dfrac{1}{6}$ _____

30. $3\dfrac{5}{7}$ _____

Using Data from a Table

Distances (km)	Philadelphia	Pittsburgh	Fort Wayne	Chicago
Philadelphia	—	565	1,080	1,318
Pittsburgh	565	—	515	753
Fort Wayne	1,080	515	—	238
Chicago	1,318	753	238	—

Solve.

1. How far is a trip from Philadelphia to Chicago?

_____

2. How far is a trip from Fort Wayne to Pittsburgh?

_____

3. How far is a trip from Pittsburgh to Chicago to Philadelphia?

_____

4. How far is a trip from Fort Wayne to Pittsburgh to Chicago?

_____

5. How much farther is it from Philadelphia to Chicago than from Pittsburgh to Chicago?

_____

6. How far is a trip from Pittsburgh to Philadelphia to Chicago and back to Pittsburgh by the same route?

_____

7. How much farther is it from Philadelphia to Pittsburgh than from Fort Wayne to Pittsburgh?

_____

8. How much farther is it from Pittsburgh to Fort Wayne than from Fort Wayne to Chicago?

_____

9. How far is a trip from Fort Wayne to Chicago to Pittsburgh and directly back to Fort Wayne?

_____

10. How far is it from Chicago to Pittsburgh, and back?

_____

Adding and Subtracting Fractions: Like Denominators

Add. Reduce to lowest terms.

1. $\frac{5}{10} + \frac{4}{10} =$ _____

2. $\frac{1}{4} + \frac{1}{4} =$ _____

3. $\frac{5}{11} + \frac{4}{11} =$ _____

4. $\frac{8}{12} + \frac{1}{12} =$ _____

5. $\frac{1}{9} + \frac{4}{9} =$ _____

6. $\frac{5}{7} + \frac{1}{7} =$ _____

7. $\frac{1}{7} + \frac{4}{7} =$ _____

8. $\frac{3}{8} + \frac{3}{8} =$ _____

9. $\frac{3}{6} + \frac{1}{6} =$ _____

10. $\begin{array}{r} \frac{2}{8} \\ + \frac{4}{8} \\ \hline \end{array}$

11. $\begin{array}{r} \frac{3}{10} \\ + \frac{5}{10} \\ \hline \end{array}$

12. $\begin{array}{r} \frac{2}{9} \\ + \frac{4}{9} \\ \hline \end{array}$

13. $\begin{array}{r} \frac{1}{6} \\ + \frac{2}{6} \\ \hline \end{array}$

Subtract. Reduce differences to lowest terms.

14. $\frac{3}{5} - \frac{1}{5} =$ _____

15. $\frac{3}{4} - \frac{1}{4} =$ _____

16. $\frac{7}{10} - \frac{2}{10} =$ _____

17. $\frac{3}{6} - \frac{2}{6} =$ _____

18. $\frac{7}{8} - \frac{5}{8} =$ _____

19. $\frac{4}{9} - \frac{2}{9} =$ _____

20. $\frac{7}{15} - \frac{6}{15} =$ _____

21. $\frac{9}{12} - \frac{7}{12} =$ _____

22. $\frac{11}{16} - \frac{7}{16} =$ _____

23. $\begin{array}{r} \frac{2}{3} \\ - \frac{1}{3} \\ \hline \end{array}$

24. $\begin{array}{r} \frac{6}{7} \\ - \frac{2}{7} \\ \hline \end{array}$

25. $\begin{array}{r} \frac{3}{4} \\ - \frac{2}{4} \\ \hline \end{array}$

26. $\begin{array}{r} \frac{4}{5} \\ - \frac{1}{5} \\ \hline \end{array}$

Name _____

Least Common Multiple

Find the least common denominator (LCD) for each pair of fractions.

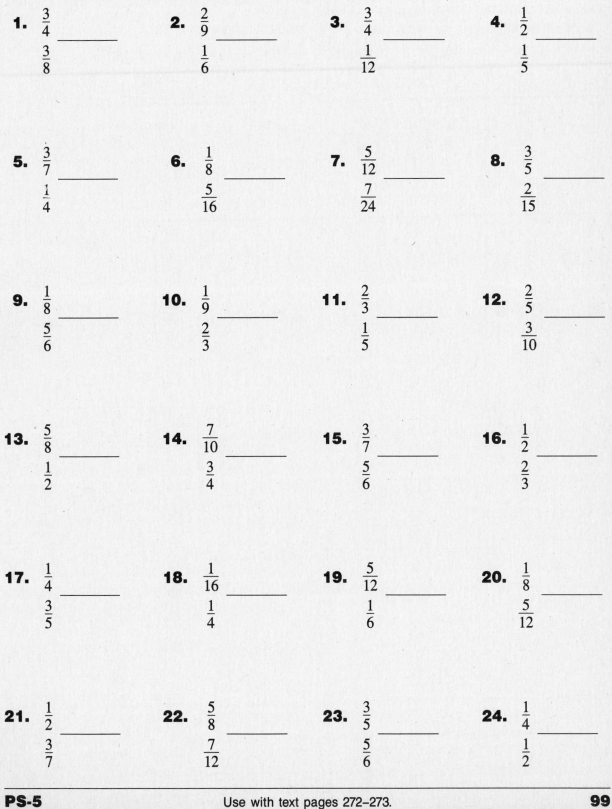

1. $\frac{3}{4}$ _____
   $\frac{3}{8}$

2. $\frac{2}{9}$ _____
   $\frac{1}{6}$

3. $\frac{3}{4}$ _____
   $\frac{1}{12}$

4. $\frac{1}{2}$ _____
   $\frac{1}{5}$

5. $\frac{3}{7}$ _____
   $\frac{1}{4}$

6. $\frac{1}{8}$ _____
   $\frac{5}{16}$

7. $\frac{5}{12}$ _____
   $\frac{7}{24}$

8. $\frac{3}{5}$ _____
   $\frac{2}{15}$

9. $\frac{1}{8}$ _____
   $\frac{5}{6}$

10. $\frac{1}{9}$ _____
    $\frac{2}{3}$

11. $\frac{2}{3}$ _____
    $\frac{1}{5}$

12. $\frac{2}{5}$ _____
    $\frac{3}{10}$

13. $\frac{5}{8}$ _____
    $\frac{1}{2}$

14. $\frac{7}{10}$ _____
    $\frac{3}{4}$

15. $\frac{3}{7}$ _____
    $\frac{5}{6}$

16. $\frac{1}{2}$ _____
    $\frac{2}{3}$

17. $\frac{1}{4}$ _____
    $\frac{3}{5}$

18. $\frac{1}{16}$ _____
    $\frac{1}{4}$

19. $\frac{5}{12}$ _____
    $\frac{1}{6}$

20. $\frac{1}{8}$ _____
    $\frac{5}{12}$

21. $\frac{1}{2}$ _____
    $\frac{3}{7}$

22. $\frac{5}{8}$ _____
    $\frac{7}{12}$

23. $\frac{3}{5}$ _____
    $\frac{5}{6}$

24. $\frac{1}{4}$ _____
    $\frac{1}{2}$

Adding and Subtracting Fractions: Making the Connection

Add or subtract. Use fraction pieces or the pictures
to rename fractions so that they have the same denominator.

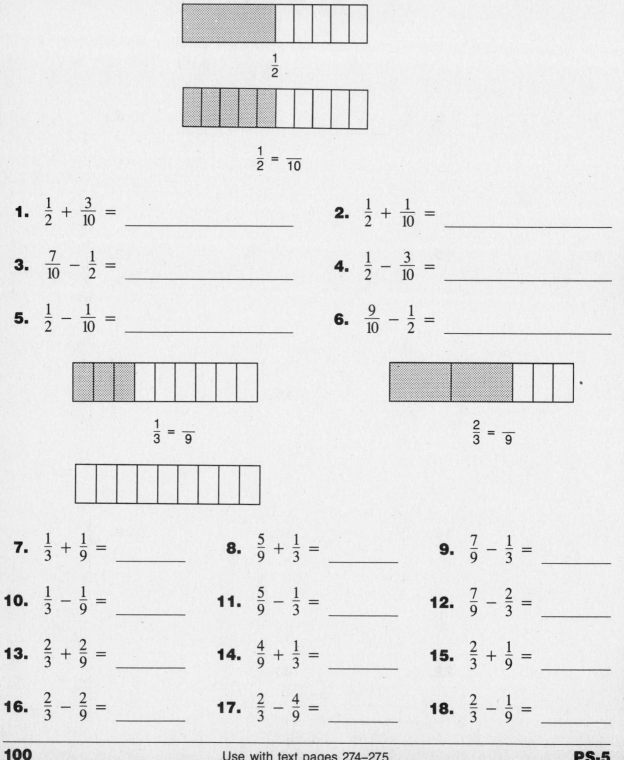

$\frac{1}{2}$

$\frac{1}{2} = \frac{}{10}$

1. $\frac{1}{2} + \frac{3}{10} =$ _____

2. $\frac{1}{2} + \frac{1}{10} =$ _____

3. $\frac{7}{10} - \frac{1}{2} =$ _____

4. $\frac{1}{2} - \frac{3}{10} =$ _____

5. $\frac{1}{2} - \frac{1}{10} =$ _____

6. $\frac{9}{10} - \frac{1}{2} =$ _____

$\frac{1}{3} = \frac{}{9}$

$\frac{2}{3} = \frac{}{9}$

7. $\frac{1}{3} + \frac{1}{9} =$ _____

8. $\frac{5}{9} + \frac{1}{3} =$ _____

9. $\frac{7}{9} - \frac{1}{3} =$ _____

10. $\frac{1}{3} - \frac{1}{9} =$ _____

11. $\frac{5}{9} - \frac{1}{3} =$ _____

12. $\frac{7}{9} - \frac{2}{3} =$ _____

13. $\frac{2}{3} + \frac{2}{9} =$ _____

14. $\frac{4}{9} + \frac{1}{3} =$ _____

15. $\frac{2}{3} + \frac{1}{9} =$ _____

16. $\frac{2}{3} - \frac{2}{9} =$ _____

17. $\frac{2}{3} - \frac{4}{9} =$ _____

18. $\frac{2}{3} - \frac{1}{9} =$ _____

Use with text pages 274–275.

Name _____

Adding and Subtracting Fractions: Unlike Denominators

Add or subtract. Reduce answers to lowest terms.

1. $\begin{array}{r} \frac{2}{3} \\ + \frac{1}{6} \\ \hline \end{array}$ **2.** $\begin{array}{r} \frac{5}{6} \\ - \frac{1}{3} \\ \hline \end{array}$ **3.** $\begin{array}{r} \frac{1}{12} \\ + \frac{3}{4} \\ \hline \end{array}$ **4.** $\begin{array}{r} \frac{4}{15} \\ + \frac{7}{30} \\ \hline \end{array}$

5. $\begin{array}{r} \frac{3}{5} \\ - \frac{2}{15} \\ \hline \end{array}$ **6.** $\begin{array}{r} \frac{1}{6} \\ + \frac{3}{5} \\ \hline \end{array}$ **7.** $\begin{array}{r} \frac{5}{6} \\ - \frac{1}{8} \\ \hline \end{array}$ **8.** $\begin{array}{r} \frac{13}{14} \\ - \frac{5}{6} \\ \hline \end{array}$

9. $\begin{array}{r} \frac{1}{6} \\ + \frac{3}{8} \\ \hline \end{array}$ **10.** $\begin{array}{r} \frac{7}{10} \\ + \frac{3}{5} \\ \hline \end{array}$ **11.** $\begin{array}{r} \frac{7}{12} \\ - \frac{1}{4} \\ \hline \end{array}$ **12.** $\begin{array}{r} \frac{1}{2} \\ - \frac{1}{10} \\ \hline \end{array}$

13. What is the sum of $\frac{5}{12}$ and $\frac{1}{4}$?   **14.** What is $\frac{3}{8}$ less than $\frac{1}{2}$?

Problems Without Solutions

If the problem has a solution, give it.
If it has no solution, explain why not.

1. Lillian's aunt said, "If you triple your own age and then subtract the product of 4 and 8, you will have my age." Lillian was 9. How old was her aunt?

_____

_____

2. Mitch said he was farther along in his book than Spencer was in his. He said, "The sum of the pages my book is open to is 132." What pages is Spencer reading?

_____

_____

3. Laurence had 5 coins. Their value was 75¢. What coins did he have?

_____

4. Persia is twice as old as her brother. The product of their ages is 72. How old is Persia?

_____

5. Rebecca found an old license plate. It had 2 letters on it and 4 digits. The sum of the digits was 44. What were the 4 digits on the license plates?

_____

_____

6. Spencer is reading a book. The product of the page numbers the book is open to is 110. What pages are they?

_____

7. Corey wanted Laura to guess what coins he had. He said, "I have three coins. The are worth exactly one-half the value of yours." If Laura's coins are worth 55¢, what coins does Corey have?

_____

_____

8. David and Anthony's houses are next to each other. The sum of their address numbers is 255. David's number is higher than Anthony's. If all of the numbers on one side of the street are odd and all of the numbers on the other side are even, what is Anthony's street number?

_____

Estimating Fraction Sums and Differences

Tom used a ruler to measure the distances between
cities on the map.

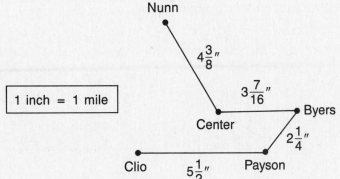

Estimate each distance in miles.

1. From Clio to Byers through Payson _____

2. From Payson to Center through Byers _____

3. From Nunn to Byers through Center _____

4. From Clio to Center through Payson and Byers _____

5. How much farther is it from Clio to Payson than
it is from Center to Byers? _____

6. How much farther is it from Nunn to Center than
it is from Byers to Payson? _____

Use the estimation method of your choice.

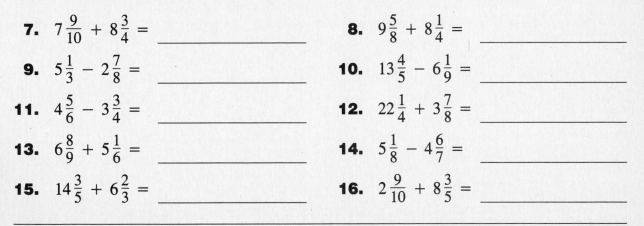

7. $7\frac{9}{10} + 8\frac{3}{4} =$ _____

8. $9\frac{5}{8} + 8\frac{1}{4} =$ _____

9. $5\frac{1}{3} - 2\frac{7}{8} =$ _____

10. $13\frac{4}{5} - 6\frac{1}{9} =$ _____

11. $4\frac{5}{6} - 3\frac{3}{4} =$ _____

12. $22\frac{1}{4} + 3\frac{7}{8} =$ _____

13. $6\frac{8}{9} + 5\frac{1}{6} =$ _____

14. $5\frac{1}{8} - 4\frac{6}{7} =$ _____

15. $14\frac{3}{5} + 6\frac{2}{3} =$ _____

16. $2\frac{9}{10} + 8\frac{3}{5} =$ _____

Name _____

Adding and Subtracting Mixed Numbers: Making the Connection

Shade the parts of the fraction pieces that are put together. Write the total.

1. $2\frac{2}{3} + 1\frac{1}{3} = $ _____

2. $1\frac{1}{4} + 2\frac{1}{2} = $ _____

3. $1\frac{1}{3} + 2\frac{1}{6} = $ _____

4. $2\frac{1}{8} + 1\frac{1}{4} = $ _____

Shade the parts of the fraction pieces that are taken away. Write how much is left.

5. $3 - 1\frac{1}{4} = $ _____

6. $3\frac{1}{3} - 2\frac{1}{6} = $ _____

7. $4\frac{1}{2} - 2\frac{1}{8} = $ _____

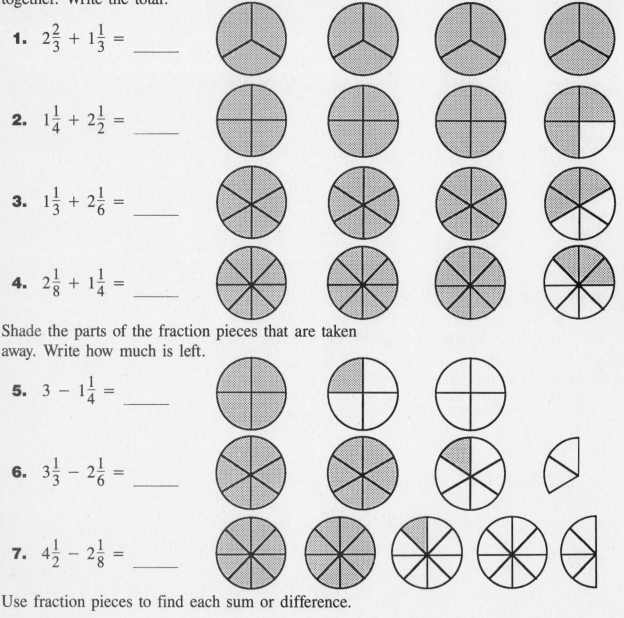

Use fraction pieces to find each sum or difference.

8. $4\frac{2}{3} + 1\frac{1}{6} = $ _____

9. $1\frac{3}{4} + 2\frac{1}{8} = $ _____

10. $5\frac{1}{2} - 2\frac{1}{4} = $ _____

11. $3\frac{1}{3} - 2\frac{1}{6} = $ _____

Name _____

Adding Mixed Numbers

Add. Reduce sums to lowest terms.

1. $2\frac{3}{5}$
     $+ 1\frac{1}{5}$
     ―――

2. $4\frac{1}{2}$
     $+ 5\frac{1}{3}$
     ―――

3. $7\frac{4}{10}$
     $+ 3\frac{1}{10}$
     ―――

4. $1\frac{1}{4}$
     $+ 3\frac{3}{8}$
     ―――

5. $3\frac{1}{2}$
     $+ 5\frac{1}{4}$
     ―――

6. $1\frac{5}{8}$
     $+ 4\frac{3}{4}$
     ―――

7. $8\frac{5}{6}$
     $+ 7\frac{2}{3}$
     ―――

8. $17\frac{1}{3}$
     $+ 23\frac{1}{6}$
     ―――

9. $41\frac{3}{4}$
     $+ 28\frac{3}{4}$
     ―――

10. $4\frac{5}{12}$
      $+ 55\frac{3}{4}$
      ―――

11. $26\frac{3}{4}$
      $+ 5\frac{1}{2}$
      ―――

12. $21\frac{7}{10}$
      $+ 88\frac{3}{5}$
      ―――

13. $46\frac{1}{2}$
      $+ 80\frac{7}{8}$
      ―――

Estimate each sum.

14. $11\frac{5}{8} + 9\frac{2}{3}$ _____

15. $3\frac{1}{3} + 6\frac{3}{4}$ _____

16. $7\frac{3}{5} + 2\frac{2}{6}$ _____

Name _____

Subtracting Mixed Numbers

Subtract. Reduce answers to lowest terms.

1. $9\frac{1}{8}$

$-\ 6\frac{5}{8}$

2. 15

$-\ 1\frac{2}{3}$

3. $6\frac{1}{5}$

$-\ 1\frac{9}{10}$

4. $10\frac{1}{2}$

$-\ 8\frac{3}{4}$

5. $8\frac{1}{4}$

$-\ 2\frac{2}{5}$

6. $7\frac{3}{8}$

$-\ 7\frac{1}{4}$

7. $223\frac{1}{2}$

$-\ 111\frac{2}{3}$

8. $19\frac{1}{4}$

$-\ 1\frac{1}{2}$

Estimate each difference.

9. $48\frac{1}{3} - 19\frac{11}{12}$ **10.** $55\frac{3}{8} - 26\frac{2}{7}$ **11.** $27\frac{2}{3} - 4\frac{4}{5}$

More Adding and Subtracting: Whole Numbers, Fractions, and Mixed Numbers

Add or subtract. Reduce answers to lowest terms.

1. $8\frac{1}{2}$
       $+ 3\frac{1}{3}$
       ‾‾‾‾‾‾‾

2. $7\frac{8}{9}$
       $- 2\frac{2}{3}$
       ‾‾‾‾‾‾‾

3. 15
       $- 6\frac{7}{10}$
       ‾‾‾‾‾‾‾

4. $25\frac{15}{16}$
       $- 4$
       ‾‾‾‾‾

5. $67\frac{11}{12}$
       $+ 12\frac{1}{12}$
       ‾‾‾‾‾‾‾

6. $56\frac{1}{2}$
       $- 22\frac{3}{7}$
       ‾‾‾‾‾‾‾

7. $\frac{9}{10}$
       $+ \frac{3}{8}$
       ‾‾‾‾‾

8. 75
       $- 6\frac{9}{14}$
       ‾‾‾‾‾‾‾

9. $288\frac{3}{4}$
       $+ 71\frac{1}{2}$
       ‾‾‾‾‾‾‾

10. $15\frac{2}{7} + 8 + 6\frac{1}{2}$

11. $5\frac{1}{2} + \frac{7}{8} + \frac{3}{4}$

Estimate each sum or difference.

12. $41 - 6\frac{7}{9}$

13. $9\frac{1}{2} + 2\frac{2}{5}$

14. $13\frac{5}{8} - 7\frac{1}{3}$

Choosing a Calculation Method

Sewing Center Sale		
Item	Length per piece	Cost per piece
Satin Ribbon	$1\frac{7}{8}$ m	$0.98
Lace	$2\frac{1}{2}$ m	$3.49
Fringe	$\frac{3}{4}$ m	$0.75
Velvet Ribbon	$1\frac{3}{4}$ m	$1.29

Use the data in the advertisement. Choose a calculation method. Solve.

1. Katherine needs $1\frac{7}{8}$ m of lace. If she buys one piece, how much will she have left over?

_____

2. William needs two pieces of fringe. One must be $\frac{2}{3}$ m long and the other $\frac{1}{4}$ m long. Can he cut both pieces from one piece of fringe?

_____

3. Alice brought a piece of satin ribbon and a piece of velvet ribbon. How much did she spend?

_____

4. Les needs $1\frac{3}{8}$ m of velvet ribbon. If he buys one piece of velvet ribbon, how much will he have left?

_____

5. Glenn bought one piece of lace and one piece of fringe. How much change should he get from $10.00?

_____

6. Mary needs a piece of satin ribbon $\frac{7}{8}$ m long and another piece $\frac{1}{2}$ m long. If she buys one piece of satin ribbon, how much will she have left over?

_____

Customary Units of Length

Change each measure to inches.

1. 2 ft 4 in. _____

2. 3 ft 6 in. _____

3. 4 ft _____

4. 1 ft 8 in. _____

5. 5 ft 5 in. _____

6. 10 ft _____

Change each measure to feet and inches.

7. 19 in. _____

8. 72 in. _____

9. 52 in. _____

10. 37 in. _____

11. 68 in. _____

12. 27 in. _____

Change each measure to yards and inches.

13. 46 in. _____

14. 180 in. _____

15. 77 in. _____

16. 112 in. _____

17. 150 in. _____

18. 182 in. _____

Write <, >, or = for each ◯.

19. 4 ft 11 in. ◯ 60 in.

20. 68 in. ◯ 6 ft

21. 2 ft 8 in. ◯ 3 yd

22. 108 in. ◯ 8 ft 2 in.

23. 72 in. ◯ 5 ft 6 in.

24. 3 yd ◯ 9 ft

25. 4 yd ◯ 144 in.

26. 10 ft 2 in. ◯ 3 yd 1 ft

27. 15 in. ◯ 1 ft 6 in.

28. 100 in. ◯ 9 ft

29. 1 yd 2 ft ◯ 60 in.

30. 5 yd ◯ 15 ft 2 in.

Length: Parts of an Inch

Measure each length to the nearest inch.

1. ├──────────────────┤   **2.** ├────────────────────────┤

_____ inches   _____ inches

Measure each length to the nearest $\frac{1}{2}$ inch.

3. ├────────────┤   **4.** ├──────────────────┤   **5.** ├────┤

_____ inches   _____ inches   _____ inch

Measure each length to the nearest $\frac{1}{4}$ inch.

6. ├────────┤   **7.** ├──────────────┤   **8.** ├────────────┤

_____ inch   _____ inches   _____ inches

Measure each length. Which measures:

9. $2\frac{1}{4}$ in.? _____   A ├────────┤

B ├──────────────────┤

10. $\frac{3}{4}$ in.? _____

C ├────────┤

11. $3\frac{5}{16}$ in.? _____   D ├──────────────────┤

E ├──────┤

12. $1\frac{7}{8}$ in.? _____

F ├────────────────────────┤

13. $1\frac{1}{8}$ in.? _____

G ├────────────────────────┤

14. $2\frac{3}{4}$ in.? _____   H ├────────────────────────┤

Name _____

Length: Feet, Yards, and Miles

Which unit would you use? Write *inches, feet, yards,* or *miles.*

1. You might drive 14 _____ to work.

2. A picnic table might be 2 _____ long.

3. A bicycle is about 5 _____ long.

4. A key is about 1 _____ wide.

5. A spoon is about 6 _____ long.

6. A bed is about 2 _____ long.

7. A refrigerator is about 6 _____ tall.

8. Alan rides his bicycle $1\frac{1}{2}$ _____ to school.

9. A telephone pole is about 30 _____ high.

10. A banana is about 8 _____ long.

11. The classroom door is about 7 _____ high.

12. Laura can run about 6 _____ in an hour.

13. A washing machine is about 1 _____ high.

Complete.

14. 24 yd = _____ ft   **15.** 3 mi = _____ ft

16. 27 ft = _____ yd   **17.** 72 in. = _____ yd

18. 8 yd = _____ in.   **19.** 10 yd = _____ ft

20. 108 in. = _____ yd   **21.** 15 yd = _____ ft

22. 10 mi = _____ ft   **23.** 75 ft = _____ yd

24. 5 yd = _____ in.   **25.** 20 mi = _____ ft

26. 39 ft = _____ yd   **27.** 144 in. = _____ yd

Problems with More Than One Answer

Find all possible answers.

1. Claire planted 36 tomato plants in her garden. How many rows did she plant? How many plants were in each row?

_____

_____

_____

2. Crystal has parakeets and dogs as pets. Altogether her pets have 16 legs. How many parakeets and how many dogs does she have?

_____

_____

_____

3. Ira and Whitney have birthdays in the same month. Ira's birthday is on the 17th. The sum of the digits of his birthdate is 8. The sum of the digits of Whitney's birthdate is 3. When is her birthday?

_____

_____

4. Juan has $0.30. What coins does he have?

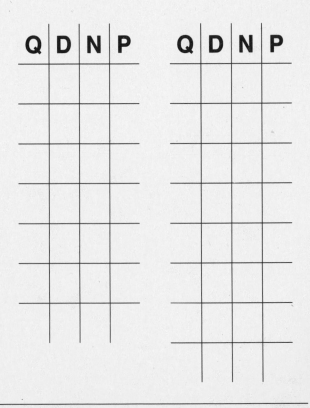

Temperature Degrees Fahrenheit

The thermometers show the normal body temperatures
of different animals. Give each temperature to the
nearest tenth.

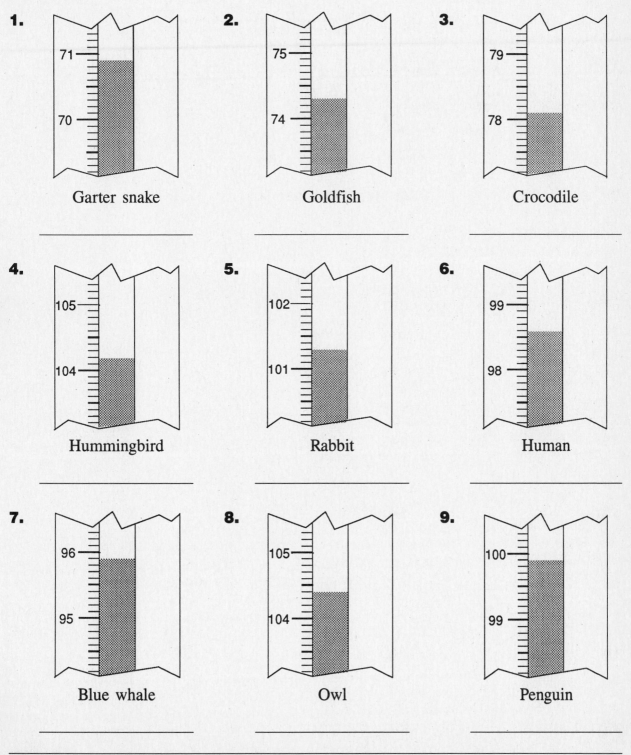

1. Garter snake

2. Goldfish

3. Crocodile

4. Hummingbird

5. Rabbit

6. Human

7. Blue whale

8. Owl

9. Penguin

Customary Units of Capacity

1 gallon (gal) = 4 quarts (qt)   1 quart (qt) = 2 pints (pt)   1 c = 8 fl oz

1 pint (pt) = 2 cups (c)   1 fl oz = 2 tbsp

Use the pictures above to complete the following.

1. 2 gal = _____ qt

2. 1 qt = _____ c

3. 2 qt = _____ pt

4. 4 gal = _____ qt

5. $\frac{1}{2}$ gal = _____ qt

6. 4 c = _____ qt

7. $\frac{1}{2}$ qt = _____ pt

8. 6 pt = _____ qt

9. 12 qt = _____ gal

10. $\frac{1}{2}$ pt = _____ c

11. 1 gal = _____ pt

12. 8 pt = _____ qt

13. 6 c = _____ pt

14. 12 pt = _____ qt

15. 8 pt = _____ gal

16. 32 fl oz = _____ qt

17. 8 fl oz = _____ tbsp

18. 6 c = _____ fl oz

19. 32 fl oz = _____ c

20. 16 tbsp = _____ c

21. 2 qt = _____ fl oz

22. 4 tbsp = _____ fl oz

23. 2 c = _____ fl oz

24. $\frac{1}{2}$ c = _____ fl oz

Customary Units of Weight

Ring the best estimate for each weight.

1. a baby

    A 10 oz

    B 10 lb

    C 10 T

2. a can of olives

    A 8 oz

    B 8 lb

    C 8 T

3. a buffalo

    A 1 oz

    B 1 lb

    C 1 T

4. a car

    A 1 oz

    B 1 lb

    C 1 T

5. a cat

    A 12 oz

    B 12 lb

    C 12 T

6. a baby bird

    A 2 oz

    B 2 lb

    C 2 T

7. a table

    A 50 oz

    B 50 lb

    C 50 T

8. a towel

    A 9 oz

    B 9 lb

    C 9 T

9. a bed

    A 150 oz

    B 150 lb

    C 150 T

Complete.

10. 3 lb = _____ oz

11. 5 lb 6 oz = ___ oz

12. 3 T 18 lb = ___ lb

13. 36 oz = _ lb _ oz

14. 4,000 lb = _____ T

15. 1 lb 9 oz = ___ oz

Write <, >, or = for each ◯.

16. 4 lb ◯ 60 oz

17. 9 lb 2 oz ◯ 144 oz

18. 19 oz ◯ 1 lb 3 oz

19. 14,000 lb ◯ 8 T

20. 1 lb 5 oz ◯ 24 oz

21. 20 lb ◯ 320 oz

Deciding When to Estimate

Tell whether you would estimate or measure.
Explain why.

1. You are going to put trim around a bookcase. Should you estimate or measure how long the strips should be?

_____

_____

2. Your class took a trip to an apple orchard. You want to tell your family how much everyone picked. Should you count or estimate the number of bushels?

_____

_____

3. Visitors want to know about how long it will take to drive from their hotel to your house. Should you measure or estimate the distance to tell how long it will take them?

_____

_____

4. You are going to put up new wallpaper in your bedroom. The pattern you have chosen is on sale because it is being discontinued. Should you measure or estimate how much you need?

_____

_____

5. Should the judges in a fishing contest estimate the weight of the catches or should they put them on the scales to find an exact weight?

_____

_____

6. You are building a cabinet that must be deep enough to hold your television set. Should you measure or estimate the depth of the television?

_____

_____

7. Your parents are buying wall-to-wall carpet for the living room. Should you estimate or measure the size of the room?

_____

_____

8. You are planting bushes in front of your house. you know about how far each bush should be from the one next to it. Should you measure or estimate where to dig the holes?

_____

_____

Name _____

Multiplying a Fraction and a Whole Number

Find the fraction of each number.

1. ○ ○ ○ ○ ○
$\overline{○ ○ ○ ○ ○}$

$\frac{1}{2}$ of 10 _____

2. ○ ○ ○ ○
$\overline{○ ○ ○ ○}$
○ ○ ○ ○

$\frac{2}{3}$ of 12 _____

3. ○|○|○|○|○
○|○|○|○|○
○|○|○|○|○

$\frac{3}{5}$ of 15 _____

4. ○|○|○|○
○|○|○|○

$\frac{3}{4}$ of 8 _____

5. ○ ○ ○
$\overline{○ ○ ○}$
○ ○ ○

$\frac{1}{3}$ of 9 _____

6. ○ ○ ○ ○ ○ ○ ○
$\overline{○ ○ ○ ○ ○ ○ ○}$

$\frac{1}{2}$ of 14 _____

Multiply.

7. $\frac{1}{4} \times 16$ _____

8. $\frac{1}{6} \times 12$ _____

9. $\frac{3}{5} \times 10$ _____

10. $\frac{1}{2} \times 24$ _____

11. $\frac{1}{10} \times 30$ _____

12. $\frac{1}{4} \times 20$ _____

13. $\frac{1}{5} \times 20$ _____

14. $\frac{2}{3} \times 6$ _____

15. $\frac{1}{2} \times 60$ _____

16. $\frac{1}{3} \times 18$ _____

17. $\frac{1}{4} \times 12$ _____

18. $\frac{3}{4} \times 24$ _____

19. $\frac{1}{5} \times 15$ _____

20. $\frac{1}{2} \times 40$ _____

21. $\frac{2}{3} \times 9$ _____

22. $\frac{3}{4} \times 8$ _____

23. $\frac{1}{6} \times 24$ _____

24. $\frac{2}{7} \times 21$ _____

Estimating a Fraction of a Number

Substitute compatible numbers to estimate each.

1. $\frac{3}{4} \times 95$ _____

2. $\frac{1}{2} \times 29$ _____

3. $\frac{2}{3} \times 26$ _____

4. $\frac{5}{8} \times 23$ _____

5. $\frac{2}{5} \times 52$ _____

6. $\frac{1}{7} \times 40$ _____

7. $\frac{1}{3} \times 58$ _____

8. $\frac{2}{9} \times 65$ _____

9. $\frac{3}{10} \times 58$ _____

10. $\frac{4}{9} \times 83$ _____

11. $\frac{1}{5} \times 37$ _____

12. $\frac{3}{8} \times 61$ _____

13. $\frac{1}{6} \times 35$ _____

14. $\frac{7}{10} \times 37$ _____

15. $\frac{4}{7} \times 47$ _____

Estimate each. Write + after the number if the exact
answer is greater than the estimate.

16. $\frac{1}{6} \times \$45.92$ _____

17. $\frac{3}{5} \times \$1.02$ _____

18. $\frac{2}{7} \times \$13.25$ _____

19. $\frac{2}{3} \times \$88.41$ _____

20. $\frac{3}{4} \times \$21.09$ _____

21. $\frac{1}{5} \times \$12.18$ _____

22. $\frac{1}{8} \times \$49.16$ _____

23. $\frac{4}{9} \times \$82.56$ _____

Multiplying Fractions: Making the Connection

1. $\frac{2}{3}$ is shaded.

Mark $\frac{1}{2}$ of $\frac{2}{3}$ with slashes.

$\frac{1}{2} \times \frac{2}{3} =$ _____

2. $\frac{4}{5}$ is shaded.

Mark $\frac{1}{2}$ of $\frac{4}{5}$ with slashes.

$\frac{1}{2} \times \frac{4}{5} =$ _____

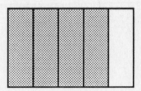

3. $\frac{3}{4}$ is shaded.

Mark $\frac{1}{3}$ of $\frac{3}{4}$ with slashes.

$\frac{1}{3} \times \frac{3}{4} =$ _____

4. $\frac{3}{4}$ is shaded.

Mark $\frac{2}{3}$ of $\frac{3}{4}$ with slashes.

$\frac{2}{3} \times \frac{3}{4} =$ _____

5. $\frac{5}{8}$ is shaded.

Mark $\frac{3}{5}$ of $\frac{5}{8}$ with slashes.

$\frac{3}{5} \times \frac{5}{8} =$ _____

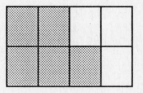

6. $\frac{5}{6}$ is shaded.

Mark $\frac{4}{5}$ of $\frac{5}{6}$ with slashes.

$\frac{4}{5} \times \frac{5}{6} =$ _____

7. $\frac{3}{10}$ is shaded.

Mark $\frac{2}{3}$ of $\frac{3}{10}$ with slashes.

$\frac{2}{3} \times \frac{3}{10} =$ _____

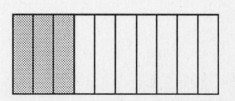

Multiplying Fractions

Multiply. Reduce to lowest terms.

1. $\frac{1}{3} \times \frac{1}{2} =$ _____

2. $\frac{1}{4} \times \frac{3}{9} =$ _____

3. $8 \times \frac{1}{4} =$ _____

4. $\frac{1}{4} \times 3 =$ _____

5. $4 \times \frac{1}{2} =$ _____

6. $\frac{2}{3} \times \frac{2}{3} =$ _____

7. $\frac{2}{3} \times \frac{1}{6} =$ _____

8. $\frac{3}{8} \times \frac{1}{7} =$ _____

9. $\frac{1}{8} \times \frac{9}{16} =$ _____

10. $\frac{3}{5} \times 10 =$ _____

11. $\frac{2}{9} \times 4 =$ _____

12. $3 \times \frac{4}{5} =$ _____

13. $\frac{2}{3} \times \frac{3}{8} =$ _____

14. $16 \times \frac{1}{8} =$ _____

15. $\frac{11}{12} \times \frac{1}{3} =$ _____

16. $\frac{3}{3} \times \frac{1}{6} =$ _____

17. $7 \times \frac{1}{21} =$ _____

18. $\frac{1}{10} \times \frac{2}{4} =$ _____

19. $4 \times \frac{1}{3} =$ _____

20. $\frac{12}{2} \times \frac{1}{4} =$ _____

Informal Algebra in Problem Solving

Draw pictures, use objects, or guess and check to
help you solve each.

1. Amanda is 21 years older than
Patricia. The total of their ages is
57. How old is Amanda?

_____

2. Carlos is half as old as Paul. If you
add their ages, you get 27. How
old is each?

_____

3. Tom is two years younger than
John. The sum of their ages is 92.
How old is each?

_____

4. If you subtract Peter's age from
Angela's, you get 20. The sum of
their ages is 52. How old is each?

_____

5. If you add Ann's age to Meredith's
age, you get 23. If you multiply their
ages you get 132. How old is each?

_____

6. Blake is 8 years older than Judy.
The sum of their ages is 12. How
old is each?

_____

7. Steven is 5 years older than
Christine. Five years from now he
will be 20. How old is Christine?

_____

8. In 6 years Megan will be 3 times
as old as David. David is 4 years
old now. How old is Megan?

_____

9. In 8 years Fran will be 21. She is
2 years older than Scott. How old
is Scott?

_____

10. One half of Terri's age is the same
as one fourth of Brian's. The sum
of their ages is 36. How old is each?

_____

Multiple-Step Problems

Solve. Show steps.

1. The fifth graders need plant food for their greenhouse. One-pound containers usually cost $4.47. They are on sale for $2.97. How much could be saved on a purchase of three pounds?

_____

_____

_____

2. At the greenhouse sale, the fifth graders charged $0.50 for a single marigold or $2.50 for 6. Mrs. Martinez bought one marigold for each of the 25 children in her class. How much did she spend?

_____

_____

_____

3. The fifth graders prepared 90 potted plants. They charged $1.50 for 1 plant or $4.00 for a group of 3 plants. What is the difference between the most the fifth graders might charge for the 90 plants and the least they might charge?

_____

_____

_____

4. Of the 112 fifth graders, $\frac{3}{8}$ prepared seedlings for the sale, $\frac{1}{2}$ prepared hanging baskets and potted plants, and the rest worked on advertising and sales. How many more students worked on plant preparation than on advertising and sales?

_____

_____

_____

5. Three fourths of the 112 fifth graders suggested that next year's class continue the project. Last year the same number of fifth graders suggested the new fifth grade continue. There were 120 fifth graders last year. What part of their class recommended going on with the project?

_____

_____

6. All 112 fifth graders visited the Botanical Gardens. They traveled by van. Each van could carry 9 students and cost $55 for the trip. How much did transportation to the Botanical Gardens cost?

_____

_____

Multiplying Mixed Numbers

Multiply. Reduce to lowest terms.

1. $2\frac{1}{6} \times 3\frac{1}{2} =$ _____

2. $2\frac{1}{4} \times 2\frac{1}{3} =$ _____

3. $5\frac{2}{3} \times 1\frac{3}{4} =$ _____

4. $3\frac{1}{9} \times \frac{1}{2} =$ _____

5. $3\frac{1}{8} \times 1\frac{1}{3} =$ _____

6. $\frac{2}{9} \times 2\frac{1}{5} =$ _____

7. $1\frac{1}{5} \times 1\frac{3}{4} =$ _____

8. $3\frac{5}{8} \times 4 =$ _____

9. $3 \times 2\frac{1}{3} =$ _____

10. $\frac{4}{5} \times 6\frac{1}{2} =$ _____

11. $\frac{5}{7} \times 3\frac{1}{3} =$ _____

12. $4 \times 2\frac{1}{2} =$ _____

13. $4\frac{1}{3} \times 1\frac{1}{3} =$ _____

14. $9\frac{1}{2} \times \frac{1}{4} =$ _____

15. $\frac{1}{2} \times 5\frac{7}{10} =$ _____

16. $4\frac{5}{6} \times \frac{1}{5} =$ _____

17. $1\frac{2}{5} \times 1\frac{7}{10} =$ _____

18. $\frac{4}{5} \times 4\frac{1}{2} =$ _____

19. $2\frac{2}{3} \times 2\frac{2}{3} =$ _____

20. $1\frac{1}{10} \times 2\frac{1}{10} =$ _____

Name _____

Using a Calculator

Solve. Use a fraction calculator.

1. Melanie has two dogs. The smaller one eats $2\frac{1}{4}$ cups of food each day. The larger one eats $1\frac{1}{2}$ times as much. How much does the larger dog eat?

_____

2. Peter is $4\frac{1}{2}$ ft tall. David is $5\frac{1}{4}$ ft tall. How much taller is David than Peter?

_____

3. A carpenter needs a piece of trim $7\frac{1}{2}$ in. long. He has a strip 9 in. long. How much trim will be left?

_____

4. Beryl cut a strip of wall paper $3\frac{1}{4}$ ft long. She then realized the wall paper needed to be $\frac{3}{4}$ of a foot longer. How long should the strip have been?

_____

5. A recipe calls for $\frac{3}{4}$ of a cup of milk. Ben is increasing the recipe $1\frac{1}{2}$ times. How much milk should he add?

_____

6. It has rained $23\frac{3}{4}$ in. so far this year. Last year at this time it had rained $25\frac{1}{8}$ in. How much more did it rain last year?

_____

7. Nancy is having a $3\frac{1}{2}$-in. photograph reduced to half size. How large will it be?

_____

8. A housepainter estimated he would need $8\frac{1}{4}$ gal of paint. He had $5\frac{1}{2}$ gal. How much more would he need?

_____

Name _____

Dividing Fractions: Using Objects and Pictures

Use fraction pieces or draw pictures to find each
quotient. Check by multiplying.

1. How many halves are in 1?

$$1 \div \frac{1}{2} = \underline{\hspace{1cm}}$$

2. How many fourths are in 1?

$$1 \div \frac{1}{4} = \underline{\hspace{1cm}}$$

3. How many fourths are in $\frac{1}{4}$?

$$\frac{1}{4} \div \frac{1}{4} = \underline{\hspace{1cm}}$$

4. How many eighths are in $\frac{1}{4}$?

$$\frac{1}{4} \div \frac{1}{8} = \underline{\hspace{1cm}}$$

5. How many thirds are in 1?

$$1 \div \frac{1}{3} = \underline{\hspace{1cm}}$$

6. How many halves are in 6?

$$6 \div \frac{1}{2} = \underline{\hspace{1cm}}$$

7. How many halves are in 3?

$$3 \div \frac{1}{2} = \underline{\hspace{1cm}}$$

8. How many halves are in 4?

$$4 \div \frac{1}{2} = \underline{\hspace{1cm}}$$

9. How many eighths are in 1?

$$1 \div \frac{1}{8} = \underline{\hspace{1cm}}$$

10. How many eighths are in $\frac{1}{2}$?

$$\frac{1}{2} \div \frac{1}{8} = \underline{\hspace{1cm}}$$

11. How many eighths are in 3?

$$3 \div \frac{1}{8} = \underline{\hspace{1cm}}$$

12. How many fourths are in $\frac{3}{4}$?

$$\frac{3}{4} \div \frac{1}{4} = \underline{\hspace{1cm}}$$

Find the quotients. Check by multiplying.

13. How many halves are in $\frac{1}{2}$?

$$\frac{1}{2} \div \frac{1}{2} = \underline{\hspace{1cm}}$$

14. How many thirds are in 2?

$$2 \div \frac{1}{3} = \underline{\hspace{1cm}}$$

15. How many fourths are in 2?

$$2 \div \frac{1}{4} = \underline{\hspace{1cm}}$$

16. How many fifths are in 2?

$$2 \div \frac{1}{5} = \underline{\hspace{1cm}}$$

17. How many sixths are in $\frac{1}{3}$?

$$\frac{1}{3} \div \frac{1}{6} = \underline{\hspace{1cm}}$$

18. How many thirds are in 3?

$$3 \div \frac{1}{3} = \underline{\hspace{1cm}}$$

19. How many fourths are in 3?

$$3 \div \frac{1}{4} = \underline{\hspace{1cm}}$$

20. How many fifths are in 3?

$$3 \div \frac{1}{5} = \underline{\hspace{1cm}}$$

Analyzing Solid Figures

Draw lines to match each space figure with its name.

Hexagonal prism

Rectangular prism

Triangular prism

Sphere

Cylinder

Cone

Triangular pyramid

Rectangular pyramid

Hexagonal pyramid

Cube

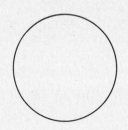
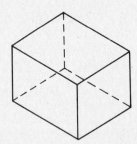

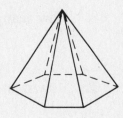
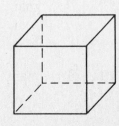
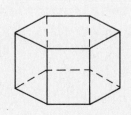
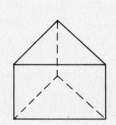

Name _____

Exploring Triangles

Write **equilateral, isosceles,** or **scalene** for each triangle.

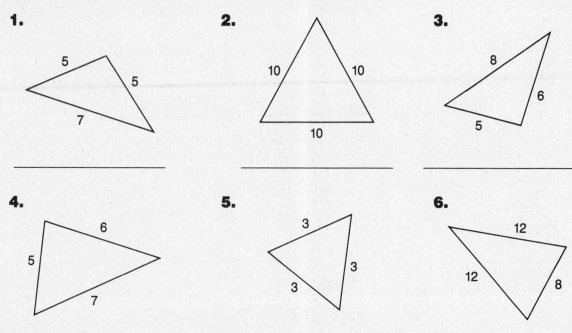

1.   **2.**   **3.**

_____   _____   _____

4.   **5.**   **6.**

_____   _____   _____

Draw the line of symmetry of each triangle. Write
none if the triangle has no line of symmetry.

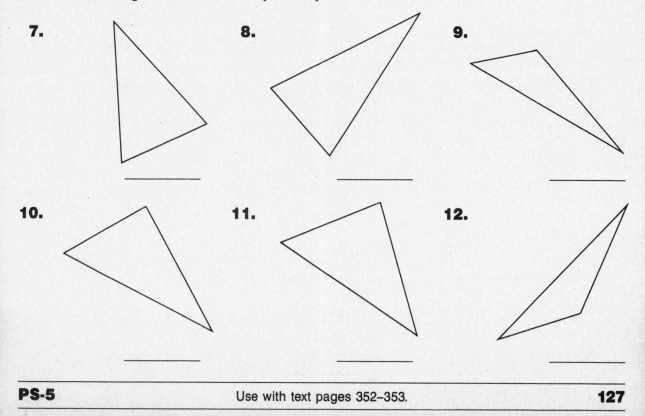

7.   **8.**   **9.**

_____   _____   _____

10.   **11.**   **12.**

_____   _____   _____

Name _____

Measuring Angles

Write the measure of each angle.

1.

2.

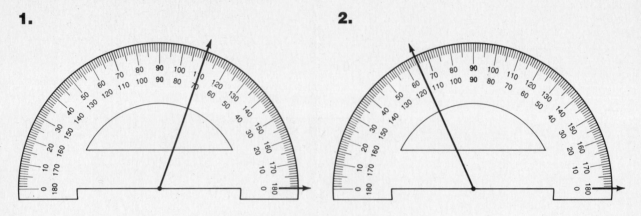

_____   _____

Estimate the measure of each angle. Then use a
protractor to check your estimate. **Estimates will vary.**

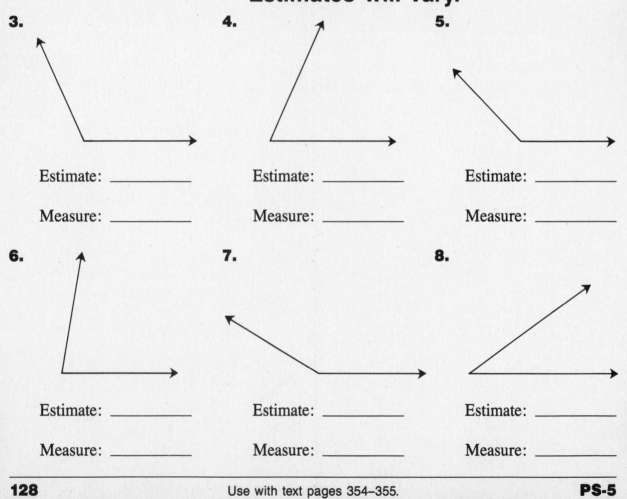

3.

Estimate: _____

Measure: _____

4.

Estimate: _____

Measure: _____

5.

Estimate: _____

Measure: _____

6.

Estimate: _____

Measure: _____

7.

Estimate: _____

Measure: _____

8.

Estimate: _____

Measure: _____

Quadrilaterals

Write **square, rectangle, parallelogram, rhombus, trapezoid** or **kite** for each quadrilateral.

Square, rhombus, or rectangle is also a parallelogram.

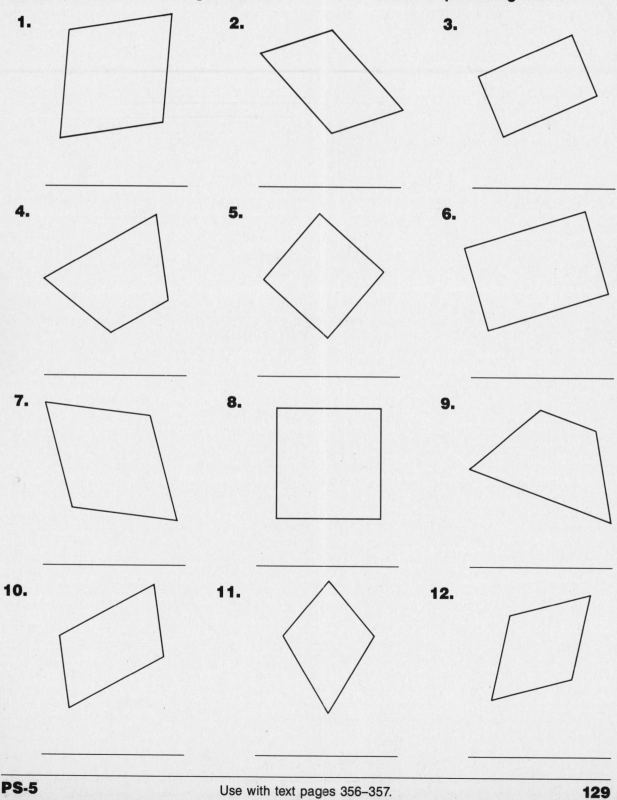

1.

_____

2.

_____

3.

_____

4.

_____

5.

_____

6.

_____

7.

_____

8.

_____

9.

_____

10.

_____

11.

_____

12.

_____

More About Quadrilaterals

Draw the lines of symmetry for each quadrilateral.
Then tell how many lines of symmetry there are for
each shape.

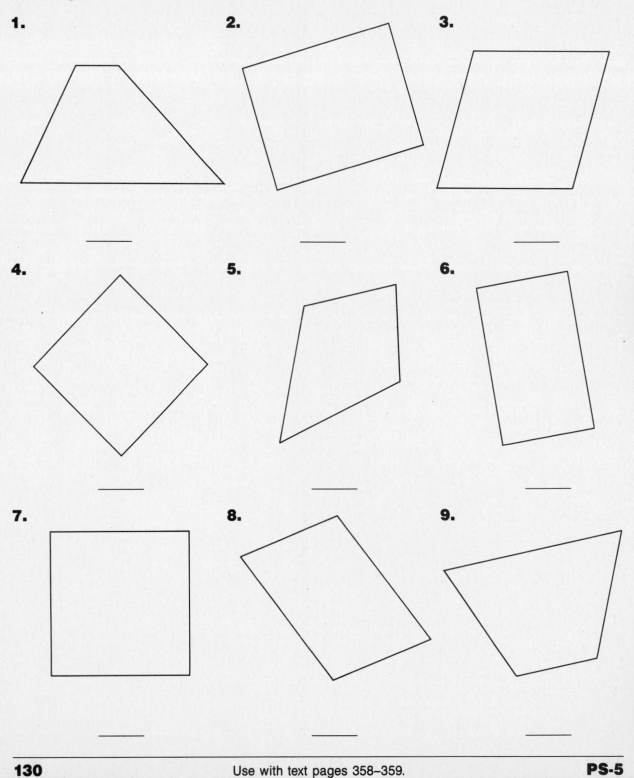

1.

_____

2.

_____

3.

_____

4.

_____

5.

_____

6.

_____

7.

_____

8.

_____

9.

_____

Using Critical Thinking

The measures of each of the angles of the triangles
below end in 0 or 5. Measure the angles and find the
sum of the angle measures of each triangle.

1.

angle A _____

angle B _____

angle C _____

sum _____

2.

angle A _____

angle B _____

angle C _____

sum _____

3.

angle A _____

angle B _____

angle C _____

sum _____

4.

angle A _____

angle B _____

angle C _____

sum _____

5.

angle A _____

angle B _____

angle C _____

sum _____

6.

angle A _____

angle B _____

angle C _____

sum _____

Based on your sums above, solve the following.

7. A triangle has a 66° angle and a 44° angle.

What is the measure of the other angle? _____

8. A triangle has a 42° angle and a 93° angle.

What is the measure of the other angle? _____

9. A triangle has a 58° angle and a 62° angle.

What is the measure of the other angle? _____

Congruent Figures and Motions

Is figure A congruent to figure B? Use tracing paper to test. Then tell which you had to do: **slide, slide and turn,** or **slide and flip.**

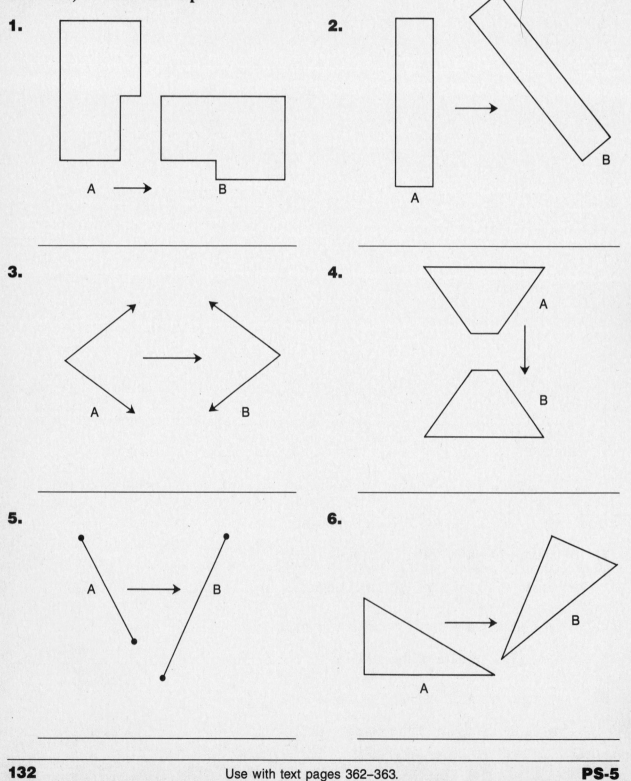

1.

A ⟶   B

_____

2.

A

B

_____

3.

A   B

_____

4.

A

B

_____

5.

A ⟶ B

_____

6.

A

B

_____

Name _____

Using Data from a Picture

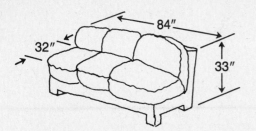

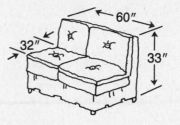

1. Does the 2-seat sofa or the 3-seat sofa allow more room per person?

_____

2. How much more room per person does it allow?

_____

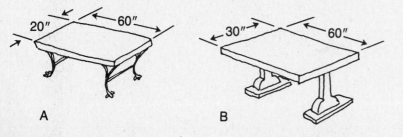

A   B

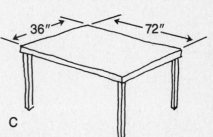

C

3. How much greater is the area of table top B than the area of table top A?

_____

4. Which is greater, the area of table top C or the combined area of table top A and table top B?

_____

5. By how many square inches is it greater?

_____

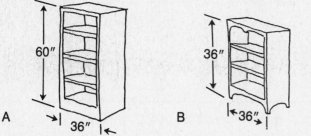

A   36"   B   36"

6. How many feet of book storage does book shelf A provide inside the frame?

_____

7. How many more inches of storage does book shelf A provide inside the frame than book shelf B?

_____

8. How many more feet of storage does book shelf A provide?

_____

Other Polygons: Tessellations

1. Shade in the tessellating triangles to create a
pattern that includes hexagons.

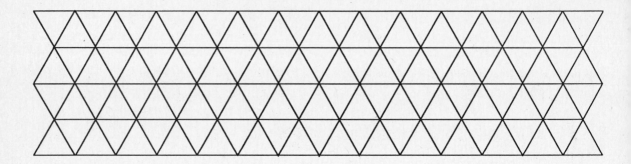

2. Shade in the triangles to create a different
pattern that includes diamonds.

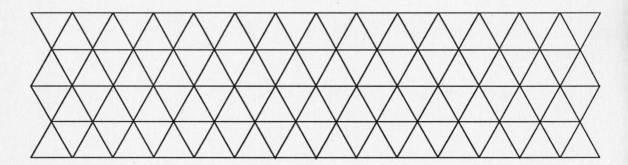

3. Shade in the tessellating squares to create a
pattern of your choice.

Circles

Label these parts of the circle:
   1. a chord
   2. a radius
   3. a diameter

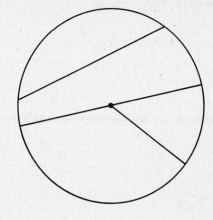

Use a compass and centimeter ruler to draw circles with these dimensions.

4. Radius 2 cm

5. Diameter 5 cm

6. Diameter 6.2 cm

7. Radius 2.6 cm

Circumference

Find the circumference. Use 3.14 for π.

1.

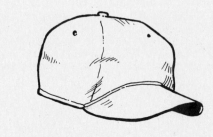

flashlight: $d = 4$ cm

$c =$ _____

2.

dog food bowl: $r = 4.5$ cm

$c =$ _____

3.

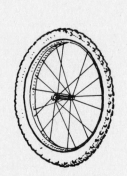

bicycle tire: $r = 28$ cm

$c =$ _____

4.

baseball cap: $d = 21$ cm

$c =$ _____

Estimate the circumference for each.

5.

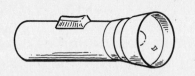

cereal bowl: $d = 14$ cm

$c \approx$ _____

6.

record: $r = 15$ cm

$c \approx$ _____

Name _____

Coordinate Geometry

Give the coordinates of each of these points.

1. A _____ **2.** B _____

3. C _____ **4.** D _____

5. E _____ **6.** F _____

7. G _____ **8.** H _____

9. I _____ **10.** J _____

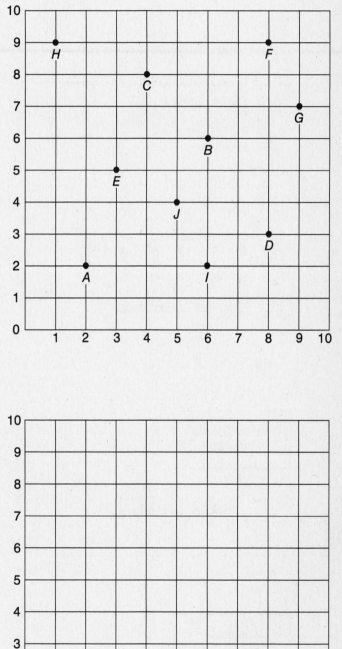

Graph each set of points. Connect the points to form a geometric figure.

11. (1,7), (2,9), (5,8), (4,6)

12. (1,3), (1,4), (2,5), (3,5),
(4,4), (4,3), (3,2), (2,2)

13. (6,5), (6,9), (8,10), (8,6)

14. (6,0), (5,2), (6,4), (8,4),
(9,2), (8,0)

Name _____

Ratio

Write each ratio in three ways.

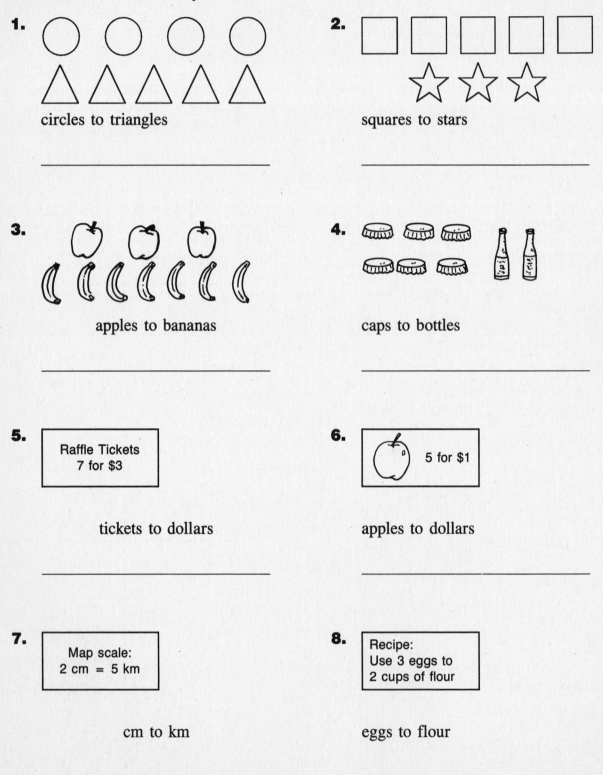

1.

circles to triangles

_____

2.

squares to stars

_____

3.

apples to bananas

_____

4.

caps to bottles

_____

5.

Raffle Tickets
7 for $3

tickets to dollars

_____

6.

5 for $1

apples to dollars

_____

7.

Map scale:
2 cm = 5 km

cm to km

_____

8.

Recipe:
Use 3 eggs to
2 cups of flour

eggs to flour

_____

Ratio Tables

Complete each ratio table.

1.

Eggs	1					
Grams of Protein	6					

2.

Potatoes	2					
Grams of Protein	8					

3.

Peaches	1					
Mg of Calcium	9					

4.

Apples	5					
Mg of Iron	2					

5.

Bananas	5					
Mg of Iron	4					

6.

Carrots	2					
Mg of Iron	1					

7.

Cups of Orange Juice	9					
Mg of Thiamin	2					

8.

Cups of Peas	2					
Mg of Niacin	5					

Write = or ≠ (not equal) for each pair of ratios.

9. $\frac{5}{2}$ ◯ $\frac{30}{12}$

10. $\frac{2}{1}$ ◯ $\frac{10}{6}$

11. $\frac{1}{9}$ ◯ $\frac{5}{54}$

12. $\frac{5}{4}$ ◯ $\frac{25}{24}$

13. $\frac{2}{8}$ ◯ $\frac{10}{40}$

14. $\frac{9}{2}$ ◯ $\frac{36}{8}$

Proportions

Solve.

1. $\dfrac{5}{6} = \dfrac{}{30}$

2. $\dfrac{2}{5} = \dfrac{}{25}$

3. $\dfrac{2}{9} = \dfrac{}{36}$

4. $\dfrac{3}{4} = \dfrac{}{24}$

5. $\dfrac{7}{8} = \dfrac{}{24}$

6. $\dfrac{1}{2} = \dfrac{}{10}$

7. $\dfrac{2}{3} = \dfrac{}{18}$

8. $\dfrac{1}{5} = \dfrac{}{40}$

9. $\dfrac{1}{3} = \dfrac{}{9}$

10. $\dfrac{7}{8} = \dfrac{}{32}$

11. $\dfrac{7}{10} = \dfrac{}{40}$

12. $\dfrac{4}{9} = \dfrac{}{18}$

Solve each problem. Use a proportion.

13. 2 out of 5 students in a class have cats as pets.. There are 20 students in the class. How many have cats?

_____

14. 3 out of 4 students in a class play a team sport. There are 28 students in the class. How many play a team sport?

_____

15. 1 out of 7 students in a class walks to school. There are 35 students in the class. How many walk to school?

_____

16. 2 out of 9 students in a class go home for lunch. There are 27 students in the class. How many go home for lunch?

_____

17. 3 out of 8 students in a class wear glasses. There are 32 students in the class. How many wear glasses?

_____

18. 3 out of 5 students in a class are boys. There are 30 students in the class. How many are boys?

_____

19. 9 out of 10 students in a class want to go on a field trip. There are 30 students in the class. How many want to go on the field trip?

_____

20. 5 out of 7 students in a class like to do ratio problems. There are 28 students in the class. How many like to do ratio problems.

_____

Using Data from a Scale Drawing

Use a centimeter ruler to measure lengths on the plan
to the nearest *tenth* of a centimeter. Then use
the scale below to solve each problem.

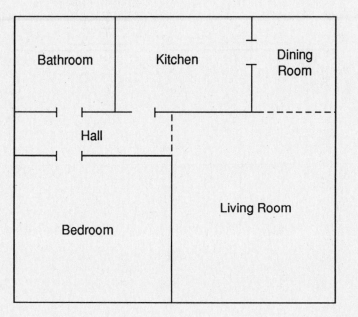

Scale:
1 cm = 1.5 m

1. What are the actual dimensions of
the bedroom?

_____

_____

2. What are the actual dimensions of
the kitchen?

_____

_____

3. What are the actual dimensions of
the bathroom?

_____

_____

4. What are the actual dimensions of
the dining room?

_____

_____

Understanding Percent

Write a ratio and a percent for the shaded part of each.

1. Ratio _____   **2.** Ratio _____

         Percent _____   Percent _____

Write each ratio as a percent.

3. 6 to 100 _____   **4.** 19 to 100 _____   **5.** 28 to 100 _____

6. 45 to 100 _____   **7.** 58 to 100 _____   **8.** 67 to 100 _____

9. 74 to 100 _____   **10.** 89 to 100 _____   **11.** 93 to 100 _____

12. $\dfrac{8}{100}$ _____   **13.** $\dfrac{96}{100}$ _____   **14.** $\dfrac{12}{100}$ _____   **15.** $\dfrac{81}{100}$ _____

16. $\dfrac{25}{100}$ _____   **17.** $\dfrac{50}{100}$ _____   **18.** $\dfrac{63}{100}$ _____   **19.** $\dfrac{39}{100}$ _____

20. $\dfrac{100}{100}$ _____   **21.** $\dfrac{71}{100}$ _____   **22.** $\dfrac{44}{100}$ _____   **23.** $\dfrac{20}{100}$ _____

Write each percent as a fraction.

24. 40% _____   **25.** 29% _____   **26.** 7% _____   **27.** 31% _____

28. 15% _____   **29.** 23% _____   **30.** 54% _____   **31.** 77% _____

32. 30% _____   **33.** 61% _____   **34.** 22% _____   **35.** 57% _____

36. 46% _____   **37.** 90% _____   **38.** 14% _____   **39.** 68% _____

40. 74% _____   **41.** 42% _____   **42.** 8% _____   **43.** 97% _____

Name _____

Percents as Decimals or Fractions

Write as a percent.

1. 0.70 _____ **2.** $\frac{38}{100}$ _____ **3.** 0.25 _____

4. $\frac{40}{100}$ _____ **5.** 0.89 _____ **6.** $\frac{6}{100}$ _____

7. 0.01 _____ **8.** 0.2 _____ **9.** 0.50 _____

10. $\frac{29}{100}$ _____ **11.** $\frac{64}{100}$ _____ **12.** 0.17 _____

13. 0.10 _____ **14.** 1.00 _____ **15.** $\frac{5}{100}$ _____

Write a decimal for each percent.

16. 54% _____ **17.** 20% _____ **18.** 3% _____

19. 19% _____ **20.** 1% _____ **21.** 40% _____

22. 76% _____ **23.** 50% _____ **24.** 10% _____

25. 9% _____ **26.** 19% _____ **27.** 100% _____

28. 33% _____ **29.** 25% _____ **30.** 7% _____

Write a fraction for each percent.

31. 60% _____ **32.** 20% _____ **33.** 3% _____

34. 75% _____ **35.** 24% _____ **36.** 10% _____

37. 19% _____ **38.** 50% _____ **39.** 1% _____

40. 40% _____ **41.** 99% _____ **42.** 25% _____

43. 12% _____ **44.** 80% _____ **45.** 45% _____

Name _____

Percents and Lowest-terms Fractions

Give the percent for each fraction.

1. $\frac{1}{4}$ _____   **2.** $\frac{2}{5}$ _____   **3.** $\frac{3}{10}$ _____   **4.** $\frac{1}{10}$ _____

5. $\frac{7}{10}$ _____   **6.** $\frac{4}{5}$ _____   **7.** $\frac{1}{2}$ _____   **8.** $\frac{10}{10}$ _____

9. $\frac{1}{5}$ _____   **10.** $\frac{9}{10}$ _____   **11.** $\frac{3}{5}$ _____   **12.** $\frac{3}{4}$ _____

Give the lowest-terms fraction for each percent.

13. 50% _____   **14.** 15% _____   **15.** 60% _____   **16.** 20% _____

17. 35% _____   **18.** 75% _____   **19.** 16% _____   **20.** 25% _____

21. 70% _____   **22.** 36% _____   **23.** 55% _____   **24.** 44% _____

Solve each problem.

25. About $\frac{9}{10}$ of the people in Ethiopia work in farming. What percent of the people is this?

_____

26. About 80% of Greenland is permanent ice and snow. What fraction of Greenland is this?

_____

27. About $\frac{3}{5}$ of Ghana's land is forest and bush. What percent of Ghana's land is forest and bush?

_____

28. About 2% of Ireland is inland water. What fraction of Ireland is inland water?

_____

Name _____

Mental Math and Estimation with Percents

Solve. Use mental math.

1. 50% of 48 _____   **2.** 20% of 55 _____

3. 10% of 90 _____   **4.** $33\frac{1}{3}$% of 24 _____

5. 40% of 80 _____   **6.** 25% of 60 _____

7. $66\frac{2}{3}$% of 18 _____   **8.** 60% of 20 _____

9. 75% of 40 _____   **10.** 100% of 92 _____

11. $33\frac{1}{3}$% of 6 _____   **12.** 25% of 4 _____

13. 80% of 50 _____   **14.** 10% of 300 _____

15. 20% of 25 _____   **16.** 40% of 15 _____

Estimate.

17. 34% of 21 _____   **18.** 10% of 199 _____

19. 75% of 398 _____   **20.** 18% of 45 _____

21. 20% of 56 _____   **22.** 26% of 400 _____

23. 62% of 25 _____   **24.** 53% of 160 _____

25. 50% of 2,003 _____   **26.** 9% of 30 _____

27. 25% of 50 _____   **28.** $33\frac{1}{3}$% of 58 _____

29. 11% of 80 _____   **30.** 12% of 900 _____

31. 24% of 40 _____   **32.** 72% of 60 _____

Name _____

Finding a Percent of a Number

Find the percent of each number.

1. 15% of 300 _____   **2.** 29% of 5,000 _____

3. 65% of 9,000 _____   **4.** 34% of 700 _____

5. 26% of 4,000 _____   **6.** 83% of 600 _____

Find the percent of each amount. Round answers to the nearest cent if necessary.

7. 80% of $250 _____   **8.** 10% of $62.13 _____

9. 65% of $92.45 _____   **10.** 45% of $90.00 _____

11. 12% of $32.15 _____   **12.** 90% of $72.18 _____

Find the amount saved.

13.

$45.00—33% off

_____

14.

$68.75—40% off

_____

15.

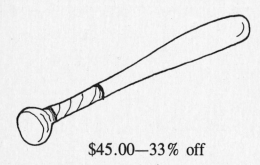

$500—10% off

_____

16.

$110.00—30% off

_____

Finding Related Problems

Solve. Tell which problem in column B can be solved in the same way as each problem in column A.

A	B

1. The librarian announced that 85% of the fourth and fifth graders had successfully completed the summer reading program. How many of the 200 students completed the program?

_____

2. Maria's questionnaire showed that 9 out of every 10 students at the Gramercy School rode bikes at least 1 day a week. Out of 500 students at the school, how many rode bikes at least once a week?

_____

3. Dario placed 3 photographs on every page of his album. He filled 16 pages. How many photographs did he use?

_____

4. There are 98 players in the baseball league. There are 8 more players in the AA division than in the AAA division. How many players are in each division?

_____

5. Justin found out that 3 out of every 5 students in his fifth-grade class watched the evening news. Out of the 35 students, how many watched the news?

_____

6. Franklin talked to 16 people who had taken their dogs to obedience classes. Only 75% thought their dogs were better behaved. How many thought their dogs' behavior had improved?

_____

7. Alina bought tennis shoes and a tennis racket. She spent a total of $96. The racket cost $24 more than the shoes. How much did each cost?

_____

_____

8. Sheri placed 20 stickers on each page of her sticker album. The album has 32 pages. How many stickers did she use?

_____

Fair and Unfair Games

1. Look at two number cubes with faces numbered 1 through 6. If you roll both cubes, how many ways can you make the sum of 2? Of 3? Of 4? Fill in the chart.

Sum	2	3	4	5	6	7	8	9	10	11	12
Number of ways											

Is the game below fair or unfair? Players roll two number cubes until there is a winner.

2. Mary wins if the sum of the roll totals 2.

   Mark wins if the sum totals 12. _____

3. Mary wins if the sum of the roll totals 7.

   Mark wins if the sum totals 9. _____

4. Mary wins if the sum of the roll totals 10.

   Mark wins if the sum totals 4. _____

Players spin 4 times each. The player with the most points wins. Is the game fair or unfair?

5. Mike wins 1 point if the pointer stops on green.

   Cole wins 1 point if it stops on yellow. _____

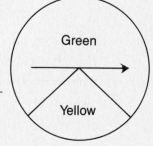

6. Mike wins 1 point if the pointer stops on green.

   Cole wins 2 points if it stops on yellow. _____

7. Mike wins 2 points if the spinner stops on green.

   Cole wins 4 points if it stops on yellow. _____

8. Mike wins 4 points if the spinner stops on green.

   Cole wins 6 points if it stops on yellow. _____

Equally Likely Outcomes

1. Spin a spinner similar to the one at the right 50 times. Keep a tally of how many times the pointer lands on an even or odd number.

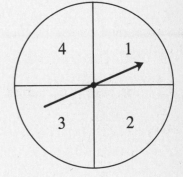

Even number	
Odd number	

Are the outcomes equally likely? _____

2. Next spin a spinner similar to the one at the right 50 times. Again keep a tally of how many times the pointer lands on an even or odd number.

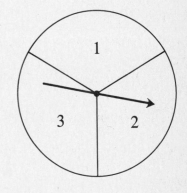

Even number	
Odd number	

Are the outcomes equally likely? _____

3. Now toss two coins 50 times. Keep a record of the outcomes in the chart below.

Coin 1: Heads, Coin 2: Heads	
Coin 1: Heads, Coin 2: Tails	
Coin 1: Tails, Coin 2: Tails	
Coin 1: Tails, Coin 2: Heads	

Is an outcome of 2 heads as likely as an outcome

of 2 tails? _____ As likely as an outcome

of 1 head and 1 tail? _____

Probability of Outcomes

Suppose this spinner is used for a game.
What are the possible outcomes if you do not
count landing on a line?

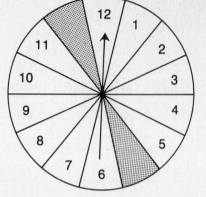

___ ___ ___ ___ ___ ___ ___

___ ___ ___ ___ ___ ___ ___

Use the same spinner to complete the exercises below.

1. $P(12) =$ _____   **2.** $P(3) =$ _____

3. $P(4) =$ _____   **4.** $P(9) =$ _____

5. P(even number) = _____   **6.** P(odd number) = _____

7. P(even or odd number) = _____   **8.** P(number < 10) = _____

9. P(number > 10) = _____   **10.** P(any number) = _____

Use the circle below.

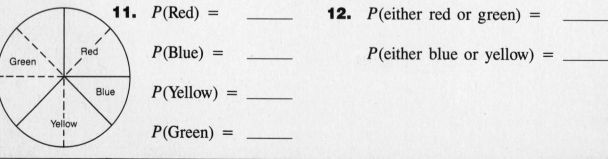

11. P(Red) = _____   **12.** P(either red or green) = _____

P(Blue) = _____ P(either blue or yellow) = _____

P(Yellow) = _____

P(Green) = _____

Name _____

Experimental and Mathematical Probabilities

Place the letters of the word *FANTASTIC* in a hat.
Pull one out, record the letter you picked, and   (F) (A) (N) (T) (A) (S) (T) (I) (C)
put it back in the hat. Try 60 pulls. Then give
the experimental and mathematical probabilities below.

Experimental Probability   Mathematical Probability

1. $P(I) =$ _____   **2.** $P(I) =$ _____

3. $P(A) =$ _____   **4.** $P(A) =$ _____

5. $P(\text{vowel}) =$ _____   **6.** $P(\text{vowel}) =$ _____

7. $P(C \text{ or } S) =$ _____   **8.** $P(C \text{ or } S) =$ _____

9. $P(\text{consonant}) =$ _____   **10.** $P(\text{consonant}) =$ _____

11. $P(T \text{ or } A) =$ _____   **12.** $P(T \text{ or } A) =$ _____

Give the mathematical probability of getting each of
the following if these six cards are turned over and
shuffled.

13. $P(\;☆\;) =$ _____   **14.** $P(\;○\;) =$ _____

15. $P(\;△\;) =$ _____   **16.** $P(\;⇧\;) =$ _____

17. $P(△ \text{ or } ○) =$ _____   **18.** $P(☆ \text{ or } △) =$ _____

Using Critical Thinking

Michael and Brett were trying to predict the winners
of this year's baseball playoffs. First they
collected the game scores for the season.

Game Scores	
King Cobras 10, Falcons 7	King Cobras 5, Falcons 2
Sting Rays 17, Lions 5	Sting Rays 7, Lions 5
Lions 6, King Cobras 5	King Cobras 9, Lions 8
Sting Rays 10, Falcons 2	Falcons 2, Sting Rays 1
Falcons 7, Lions 1	Lions 1, Falcons 0
Sting Rays 1, King Cobras 0	Sting Rays 7, King Cobras 2

1. Complete the table of wins and losses for each team.

Team	Wins	Losses
King Cobras	_____	_____
Falcons	_____	_____
Sting Rays	_____	_____
Lions	_____	_____

2. Use these statistics to predict the winner and the runner-up of the playoffs.

_____

3. Do you think it is likely or certain that these teams will win? Explain.

_____

_____

_____

_____

Name _____

Using Data from an Order Form

Suzanne runs a water sports camp. She needs
the following equipment for her canoeing
program: 2 Explorer and 1 Rapid-Racer
canoes, 8 paddles, and 16 youth water vests.
Use the price list to fill in the order form
below. Remember to include tax and shipping
in your total. Suzanne will pay by check.

River Sports, Inc.

#165 Explorer Canoe—$450.00*	Water Vest
#176 Rapid-Racer Canoe—$498.00*	#14 Standard—$35.95
#55 Folding Boat Cart—$145.00	#13 Youth —$32.95
	#45 Canoe Paddle—$15.50
*$50 shipping charge each	

ITEM NO.	Quantity	Description	Item Amount
_____	_____	_____	_____
_____	_____	_____	_____
_____	_____	_____	_____
_____	_____	_____	_____
_____	_____	_____	_____

Payment Method

Check _____   Charge _____   Item Total   _____

6% Sales Tax   _____

Shipping   _____

Total   _____

Name _____

Making Estimates by Sampling

City officials needed to estimate how many people use Warren Park at different times. First they estimated that 3 people came to the park in each car. Then they took a sample of the number of cars parked at three different times over a 5-day period. The results are shown in the table below.

	Wednesday	Thursday	Friday	Saturday	Sunday
Cars at 9 a.m.	22	20	18	12	8
Cars at 1 p.m.	44	52	68	86	40
Cars at 5 p.m.	35	40	51	46	48

1. What was the mean number of cars parked

at 9 a.m.? _____

at 1 p.m.? _____

at 5 p.m.? _____

2. What was the median number of cars parked

at 9 a.m.? _____

at 1 p.m.? _____

at 5 p.m.? _____

3. Estimate the number of people at Warren Park based on the mean number of cars parked

at 9 a.m. _____

at 1 p.m. _____

at 5 p.m. _____

4. Estimate the number of people at Warren Park based on the median number of cars parked

at 9 a.m. _____

at 1 p.m. _____

at 5 p.m. _____

Use with text pages 422–423.

Name _____

Simulations

Stu forgot to study for a math test. There were 16
questions on the test and each question had three
possible answers. Stu got only 8 right.

"I might as well have made random guesses," he
said. Is this true? How many questions do you think
he would have answered correctly by guessing?

Try the following simulation to model the situation.
Roll a number cube with 1 to 6 dots on it. A roll of
1 or 2 dots represents A, 3 or 4 dots represents B,
and 5 or 6 dots represent C. Record the result in the
first open space in the column labeled *Guessed
Answer* in the chart below. Repeat until the chart
is completed. Then count the number of times the
guessed answer matched the actual answer.

Problem Number	Actual Answer	Guessed Answer	Problem Number	Actual Answer	Guessed Answer
1	C		9	B	
2	A		10	C	
3	A		11	B	
4	B		12	A	
5	C		13	A	
6	B		14	C	
7	A		15	B	
8	C		16	C	

Name _____

Perimeter

Find the perimeter of each figure.

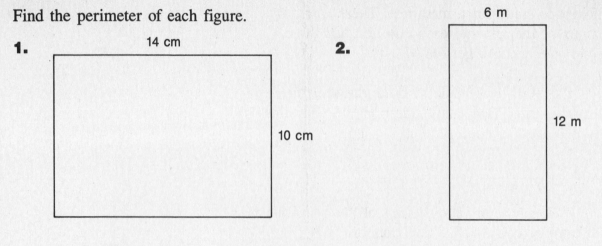

1.

14 cm

10 cm

Perimeter _____

2.

6 m

12 m

Perimeter _____

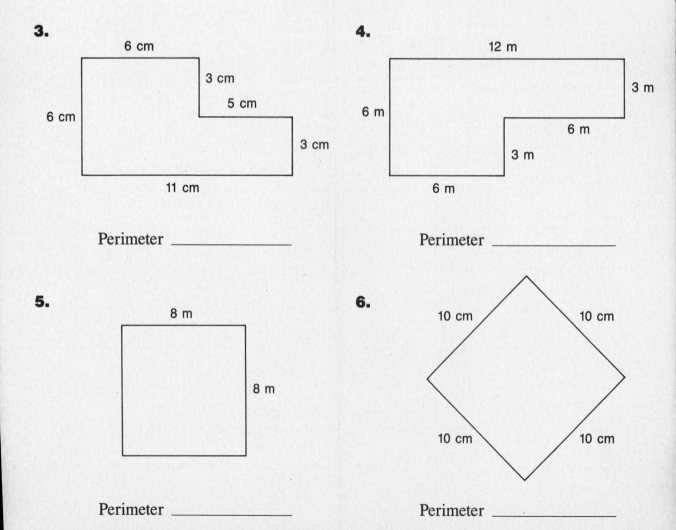

3.

6 cm

3 cm

6 cm

5 cm

3 cm

11 cm

Perimeter _____

4.

12 m

6 m

3 m

6 m

3 m

6 m

Perimeter _____

5.

8 m

8 m

Perimeter _____

6.

10 cm   10 cm

10 cm   10 cm

Perimeter _____

Estimating the Answer

Before solving each problem, estimate the answer.
Then solve the problem and decide whether your answer
is reasonable.

1. Mrs. Howard plans to take Rachel
and two of Rachel's friends to the
movies. Tickets cost $3.50. Juice
costs $1.50 and popcorn costs $2.00.
Tax on the juice and popcorn is 7%.
Mrs. Howard plans to buy a ticket,
one juice, and one popcorn for each
girl and herself. How much money
does she plan to spend?

_____

2. Mr. Bernie wanted to be sure the
chairs at the store would fit at his
table. Each chair was 42 cm wide.
He needed 6 chairs. What was the
least amount of space they require
to fit around the table?

_____

3. Mr. Bernie built a table 103 cm long
and 89 cm wide. What was the
perimeter?

_____

4. The perimeter of the dining room is
55 ft. The length is $15\frac{1}{4}$ ft. What
is the width?

_____

5. At the library 25% of the books
returned are overdue. One day 372
books were returned. How many
were overdue?

_____

6. The library charged $0.12 for each
day a book was late. How much did
Ralph pay when he brought back
three books that were 11 days late?

_____

7. Emma purchased 6 dictionaries for
the library. The total cost was
$47.34. How much did each cost?

_____

8. John ran 3.3 miles 4 times a week
for 5 weeks. How far did he run?

_____

Area of Figures with Irregular Shapes

Find the total area of each figure.

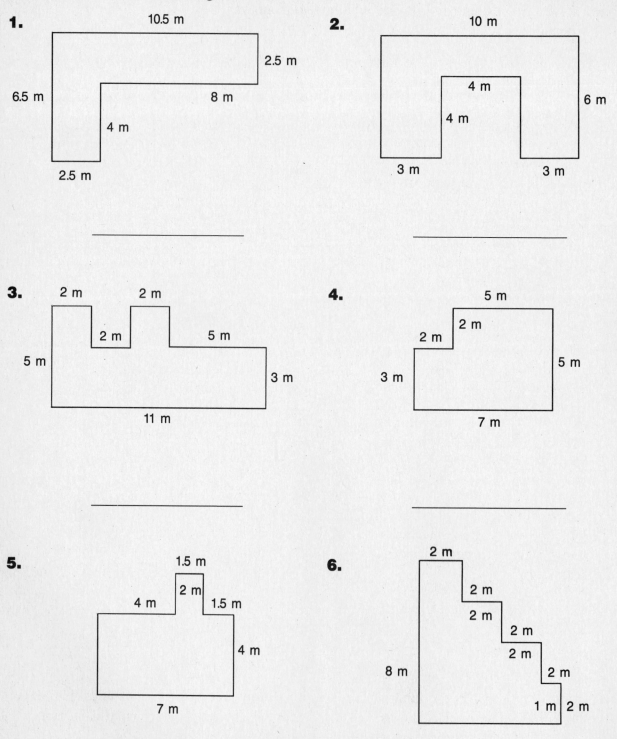

1.

10.5 m

2.5 m

6.5 m   8 m

4 m

2.5 m

_____

2.

10 m

4 m

4 m   6 m

3 m   3 m

_____

3.

2 m   2 m

2 m   5 m

5 m   3 m

11 m

_____

4.

5 m

2 m

2 m   5 m

3 m

7 m

_____

5.

1.5 m

2 m

4 m   1.5 m

4 m

7 m

_____

6.

2 m

2 m

2 m

2 m

2 m

8 m   2 m

1 m   2 m

_____

Using Critical Thinking

Find the perimeter and area for each figure.

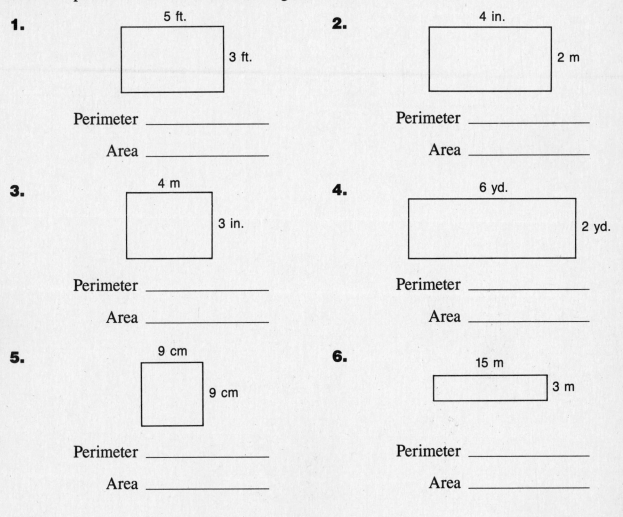

1.

5 ft.

3 ft.

Perimeter _____

Area _____

2.

4 in.

2 m

Perimeter _____

Area _____

3.

4 m

3 in.

Perimeter _____

Area _____

4.

6 yd.

2 yd.

Perimeter _____

Area _____

5.

9 cm

9 cm

Perimeter _____

Area _____

6.

15 m

3 m

Perimeter _____

Area _____

Solve.

7. A rectangle has an area of 18 m² and a perimeter of 18 m. What are its length and width?

_____

8. A rectangle has an area of 24 cm² and a perimeter of 22 cm. What are its length and width?

_____

9. A square has a perimeter of 20 m. What is its area?

_____

Area of Right Triangles

Give the height, base, and area of each right
triangle. Each □ = 1 square unit.

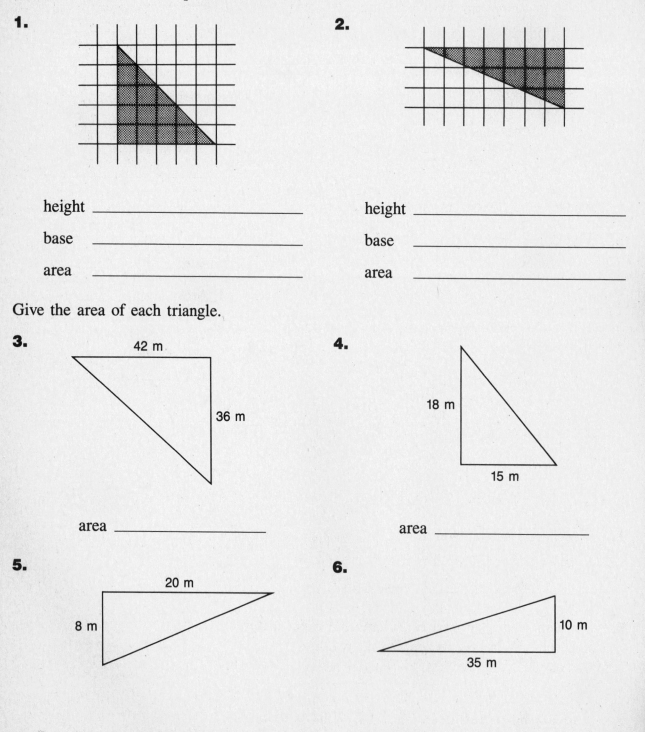

1.

height _____

base _____

area _____

2.

height _____

base _____

area _____

Give the area of each triangle.

3.

42 m

36 m

area _____

4.

18 m

15 m

area _____

5.

20 m

8 m

area _____

6.

10 m

35 m

area _____

More About Area of Triangles

Give the height, base, and area of each right
triangle. Each □ = 1 square unit.

1.

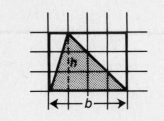

2.

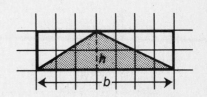

height _____   height _____

base _____   base _____

area _____   area _____

Give the area of each triangle.

3.

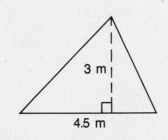

3 m

4.5 m

area _____

4.

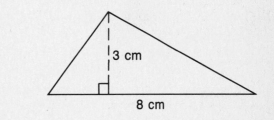

3 cm

8 cm

area _____

5.

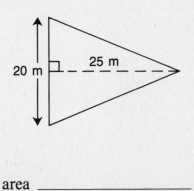

20 m   25 m

area _____

6.

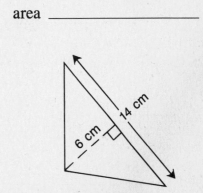

6 cm   14 cm

area _____

Area of Parallelograms

Give the height, base, and area of each parallelogram.

1.

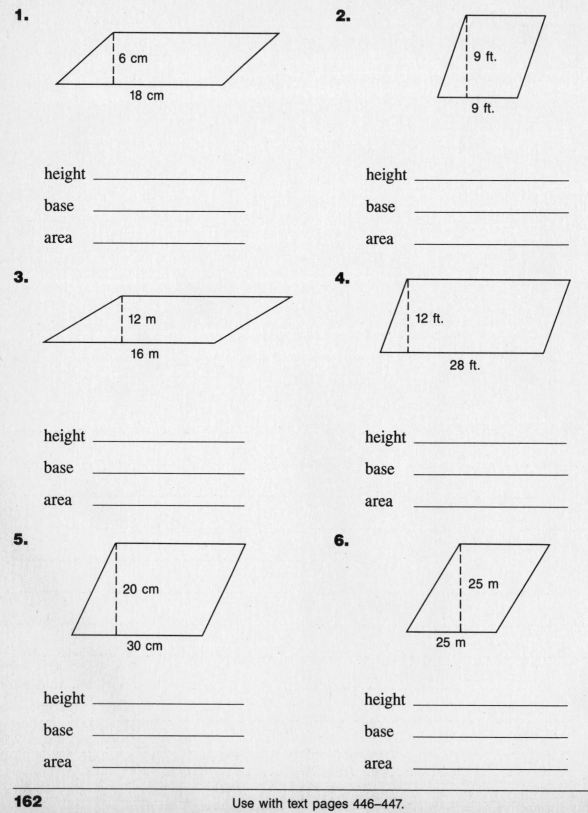

6 cm

18 cm

height _____

base _____

area _____

2.

9 ft.

9 ft.

height _____

base _____

area _____

3.

12 m

16 m

height _____

base _____

area _____

4.

12 ft.

28 ft.

height _____

base _____

area _____

5.

20 cm

30 cm

height _____

base _____

area _____

6.

25 m

25 m

height _____

base _____

area _____

Name _____

Volume

Complete the table below for each box shown.

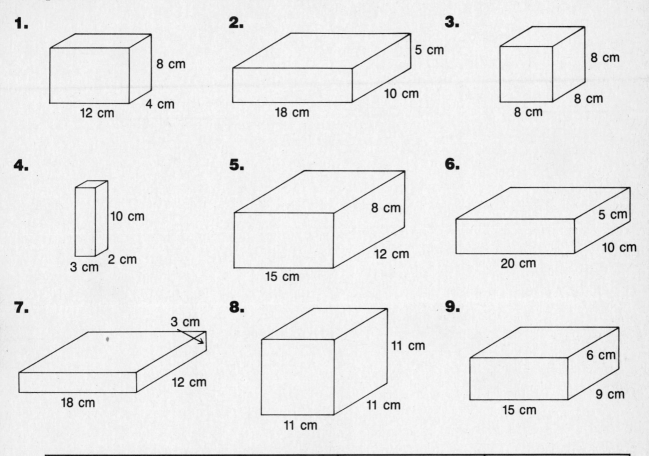

1. 8 cm, 4 cm, 12 cm

2. 5 cm, 10 cm, 18 cm

3. 8 cm, 8 cm, 8 cm

4. 10 cm, 2 cm, 3 cm

5. 8 cm, 12 cm, 15 cm

6. 5 cm, 10 cm, 20 cm

7. 3 cm, 12 cm, 18 cm

8. 11 cm, 11 cm, 11 cm

9. 6 cm, 9 cm, 15 cm

	Length (cm)	Width (cm)	Height (cm)	Volume (cm³)
1.				
2.				
3.				
4.				
5.				
6.				
7.				
8.				
9.				

PS-5

Name _____

Surface Area

Complete the table to find the surface area for
each box shown. Use a calculator if needed.

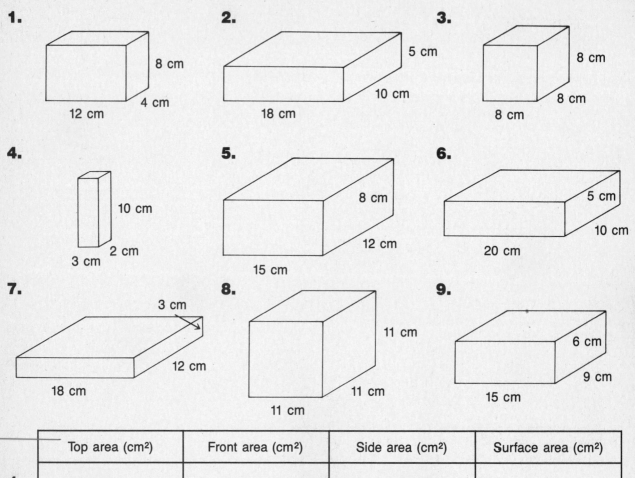

1. 8 cm, 12 cm, 4 cm

2. 5 cm, 10 cm, 18 cm

3. 8 cm, 8 cm, 8 cm

4. 10 cm, 2 cm, 3 cm

5. 8 cm, 12 cm, 15 cm

6. 5 cm, 10 cm, 20 cm

7. 3 cm, 12 cm, 18 cm

8. 11 cm, 11 cm, 11 cm

9. 6 cm, 9 cm, 15 cm

	Top area (cm²)	Front area (cm²)	Side area (cm²)	Surface area (cm²)
1.				
2.				
3.				
4.				
5.				
6.				
7.				
8.				
9.				